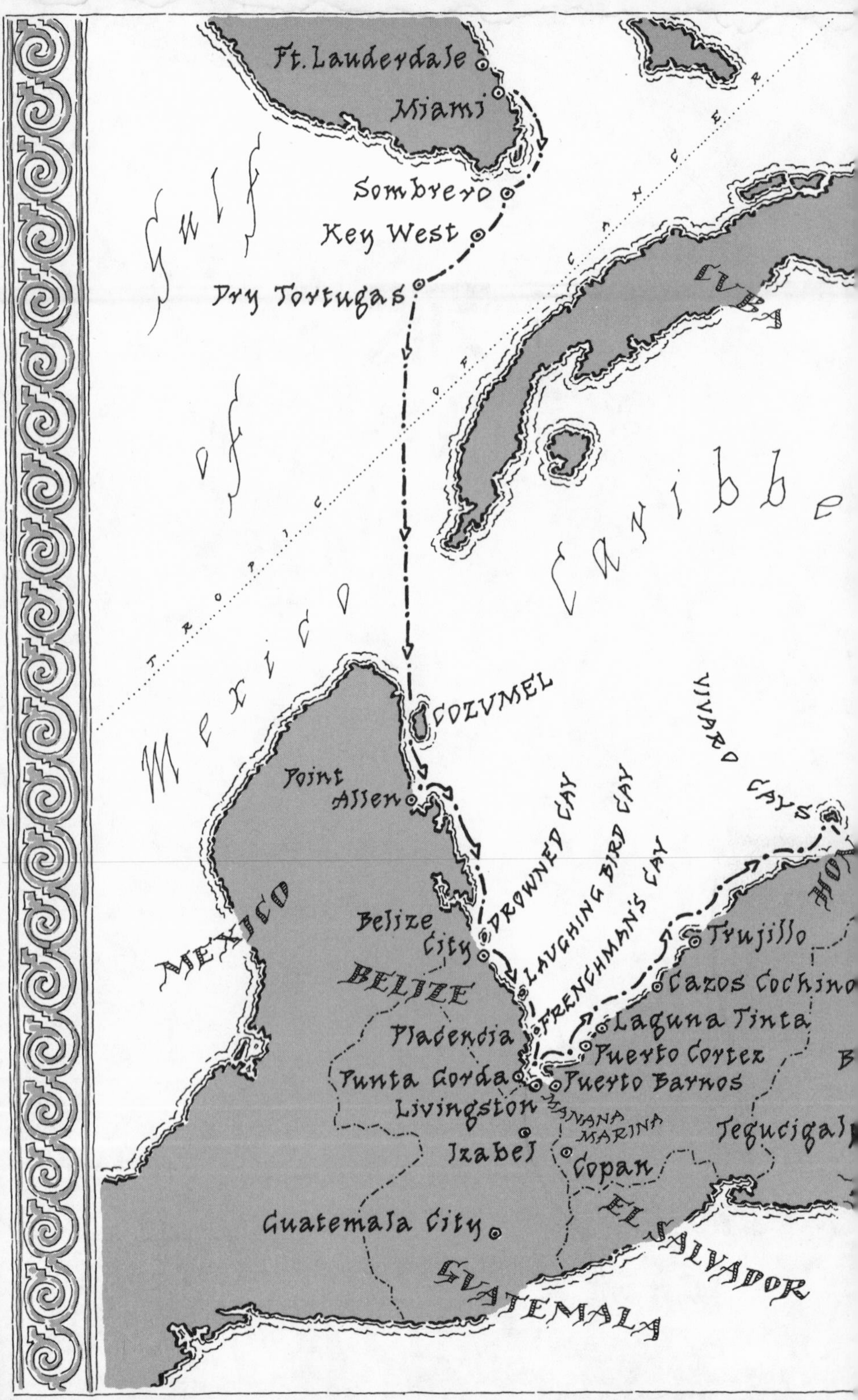
Ft. Lauderdale
Miami
Sombrero
Key West
Dry Tortugas
Gulf of Mexico
TROPIC OF CANCER
CUBA
Caribbe
COZUMEL
Point Allen
VIVARO CAYS
DROWNED CAY
LAUGHING BIRD CAY
FRENCHMAN'S CAY
Belize City
BELIZE
MEXICO
Trujillo
Cazos Cochino
Laguna Tinta
Placencia
Puerto Cortez
Punta Gorda
Puerto Barnos
Livingston
MANANA MARINA
Izabel
Copan
Tegucigal
Guatemala City
EL SALVADOR
GUATEMALA

© 1992 Oliver Williams
Boat courtesy of Susan Atkinson

JAMAICA

SEA

N

SAN
BLAS

uerto Lempira
Puerto Viejo
Puerta
Cabeza

GREAT CORN ISLAND

PANAMA

Playa Blanca

COLON

CANAL

fields   El BLUFF

Boca
del Toro

Pedro Miguel
Boat Club

Puerto Limon
San Jose

PANAMA

COSTA
RICA

AGUA

Kilometers
Miles

0   50 100   200   300   400

0   50   100   150   200   250

OTHER BOOKS IN THE DESTINATIONS SERIES
Introductions by Jan Morris

Alice Adams
Mexico:
Some Travels and Some Travelers There

Fergus M. Bordewich
Cathay:
A Journey in Search of Old China

M. F. K. Fisher
Long Ago in France:
The Years in Dijon

Herbert Gold
Best Nightmare on Earth:
A Life in Haiti

Thomas Keneally
The Place Where Souls Are Born:
A Journey Into the Southwest

Aaron Latham
The Frozen Leopard:
Hunting My Dark Heart in Africa

William Murray
The Last Italian:
Portrait of a People

Mary Lee Settle
Turkish Reflections:
A Biography of a Place

A DESTINATIONS BOOK

The Fever Coast Log

Gordon Chaplin

INTRODUCTION BY JAN MORRIS

A TOUCHSTONE BOOK
Published by Simon & Schuster
New York   London   Toronto   Sydney   Tokyo   Singapore

In memory of my father

TOUCHSTONE
Simon & Schuster Building
Rockefeller Center
1230 Avenue of the Americas
New York, New York 10020

Copyright © 1992 by Gordon Chaplin

1   3   5   7   9   10   8   6   4   2

Library of Congress Cataloging-in-Publication Data is
available

ISBN 0-671-76123-4
ISBN 0-671-76729-1 (pbk)

Contents

Introduction by Jan Morris ix

ONE: Belize 1

TWO: Guatemala 53

THREE: Honduras 97

FOUR: Nicaragua 155

FIVE: Reprise: Points South 205

Coda 221

Selected Bibliography 227

Acknowledgments

This book definitely would not have been possible without the following persons: Susan Atkinson (who will need no introduction); my agent Esther Newberg; my editor Marilyn Abraham; and last but not least my advisor Mary D. Edsall. I'm not sure whether it is a coincidence that they happen to be women.

Introduction
by Jan Morris

No doubt about it, the ultimate travel is travel by sea, in one's own small boat, in good company, with interesting purposes in mind, in some little-known and intriguing part of the world's oceans. Then even the method of locomotion becomes fascinating, elevated as it is by the navigational arts and the skills of self-preservation, while the most desolate or prosaic shoreline, seen from the deck of a yacht after long days at sea, acquires a spacious glamour. It is exciting enough to discover the coast of Spain, say, from the promenade deck of a cruise ship: Imagine what it must be like to sight the dim lights of the Fever Coast from the cockpit of a thirty-five-foot Dutch-built motorcruiser named the *Lord Jim,* as one loiters through the sweltering tropics with one's love of the day!

This is just what Gordon Chaplin does, in this spiced and evocative book. It is an almost archetypal travel book. Mr. Chaplin sets out with his friend Susan not on one, but on several quests. He is in search of himself—virtually a *sine qua non,* it seems, of contemporary American travel writing. He is in search of memories of his relative Frederick Catherwood, a wandering artist of the nineteenth century. He is searching in a more subtle way for revelations of his own father's influence and personality. It goes without saying that he is on the lookout for adventure. And he is pining for an evasive, compelling, pungent, and perhaps threatened abstraction which he calls seediness—the run-down cynical flavor of life, preferably experienced in tropical climes in politically shaky republics, which Graham Greene has made his own.

Where better to pursue seediness than along the Fever Coast, the seldom-visited Atlantic coastline of Belize, Guatemala, and Honduras—banana country, CIA country, skulldug-and-dictator country, Greene country in fact, where seediness is part of the very genius of the place? In the course of his several purposes Mr. Chaplin finds seediness with a vengeance, but he also discovers, among the shacks, the slums, the mission houses, the customs offices, the hurricane-blasted anchorages and the sleazy taverns, every kind of surprise. He is your perfect seren-dipitous traveller, because although by no means all his casual discoveries are happy ones, there is nothing that does not interest him, and hardly anything from which he does not draw lessons, conclusions, and comforts.

The cruise was not easy. Calamities of many kinds befall the voyagers. The author's spirits rise and fall. There are moments when the promenade deck of that cruise ship feels infinitely preferable to the tossing fantail of the *Lord Jim*. But there is an air of triumph to the tale, too. The boat did not sink, the two voyagers survived the stresses of an all-too-close companionship, and Mr. Chaplin found most of the things he wanted to find. Once again the quality of seediness, like garden compost, has proved creative, and the Fever Coast has produced a work of paradoxically temperate fulfillment—to quote W. H. Auden, "where hearts meet and are really true."

One

Belize

*W*E WERE keyed up from lack of sleep, too much Mexican coffee, and the strange childlike feeling of undifferentiated promise you get with every new landfall. The water was calm and silky and reflected the newly risen sun so the reef would be impossible to see until you were right on top of it. The barrier reef was 100 miles long and rose almost straight from open ocean to within six inches of the surface. It had been wrecking boats since the 1500s, helping to make Belize what it is now. Or what it is not.

We felt our way in at two knots, Susan on the bowsprit looking for coral heads. A quarter of a mile to the south, the English Cay light pushed rustily from a postcard cluster of palms and white sand and seemed to be about where it should be. The amber digital numerals on the Fathometer went from 800 to 30 in a flash. Susan roared. We turned hard port. They dropped to 200 just as quickly, then eased up to 100 and held steady as we found the channel.

Ahead of us was a huge lagoon with green islands riding on a mirage somewhere between the water and the sky, low hills over the western horizon, the higher mountains of Central America poking out of the haze to the south. An egret landed on the mizzen and stood dauntingly still. The lagoon was ornamented with inappropriate white sails that made it appear like Biscayne

Bay. Nothing seemed real. We'd had a fight about something at sundown and barely talked all night changing watches. Now talk didn't feel appropriate either.

The water changed from dark blue to light blue to green and then to khaki. The channel writhed in a peculiarly disorienting way. And on the thin pencil line of horizon, the seedy red tin roofs of Belize City began to realize themselves from their reflections.

W E ANCHORED in shallow brown water off a long wooden pier extending from one of the two buildings higher than two stories. Strings of darker brown algae zipped past on a strong outgoing tide. There was still no wind, and as soon as we stopped moving the heat wrapped around us like a rubber blanket. The heat was much stronger than in Punta Allen in the Yucatan. It was much stronger than in Cozumel, Key West, or Fort Lauderdale, where we'd set sail three weeks earlier. It was real Central American heat at last.

We set our whiskey staysail over the cockpit against the buzzing sun, poured the last of our cold coffee, and scanned the shore with field glasses . . . in one of the two buildings higher than two stories, of discolored stone, people were sitting behind bars staring back at us. It turned out to be the jail. The other one with the pier was a hotel. The rest of the buildings we could see were wood, set on pilings, with every extension and veranda at a slightly different angle. They didn't look solid enough for either tourists or prisoners.

We were flying a yellow quarantine flag to show we had just arrived from abroad, and wondering about entry procedures. Our thirty-six-foot motorsailer seemed to be the only "pleasure craft" around. The limp sails floating through the airy mirage near the horizon turned out to belong to fishing smacks and sand lighters. A few beat-up shrimp boats and freighters were anchored to their reflections farther out in the open lagoon. A beautiful old launch that looked kind of presidential in a turn-of-the-century way was towing the becalmed lighters in one by one. The smoke from its tall stack went straight up into the sky.

"*Lord Jim,* this is *Dulce.* Do you copy?" The VHF was spitting at us.

I never did get used to being called Lord Jim, even in six months of sailing down the entire lost, forgotten Caribbean coast of Central America . . . Lord Jim, Joseph Conrad's most uncompromisingly romantic hero who had chosen precisely this type of venue in which to bury himself and the memory of his terrible mistake . . .

"*Lord Jim* . . . is that you?"

No, it's not me. Far from it. I didn't even name the boat. The original owners, improbably romantic Germans who loved Conrad . . . it was their idea, and now I was stuck with it. To change a boat's name is bad luck. If I'd had the chance, I would have named her the *Urchin* or the *Susan.* Something a little more down to earth. She's certainly not romantic-looking: a stubby, short-rigged motorsailor designed after fishing smacks in the North Sea and built by the stolid, practical Dutch.

Still, I have to admit that this trip we'd planned for her fit the name a little. It had started of course with a personal tragedy . . . more mundane than Lord Jim's was, but in its own gray crushing way maybe worse.

A process of elimination over the years had led me to believe I was a writer . . . I even began to think that sooner or later I would get the recognition I deserved. This thinking persisted as "later" became more and more obviously the operative word: I had been late-blooming in other things, too. So in spite of a few gray hairs and lower back trouble, I kept the faith.

Then gradually I found myself trapped in the tunnel of an uninspired novel filled with mean characters I had come to hate but had to face every day until even they decided it was useless to go on. It wasn't a shattering failure . . . just a narrowing down, as the light at the end receded and finally faded out completely. I was left with not a whole lot of confidence or hope and no sense anymore of who I was and what I was supposed to be doing. But I didn't feel like burying myself just yet.

In the early mornings I'd been feeling okay. Maybe that was the hardest part: Almost every day carried with it all the old promise. But in three hours at the outside (I timed it) things would start narrowing down. By ten o'clock I'd be back in that gray tunnel again. Middle age had something to do with it, too.

There was a scene in an Ingmar Bergman movie I couldn't get out of my mind. An old man (or possibly woman) was talking . . . maybe to a child. About sensation. He or she was losing the feel of things. When he ran his fingers over them they made no particular impression on his mind. A piece of rough wood, a lock of hair, skin: It was all becoming undifferentiated.

I have always had a possibly naive and quite American belief in the tonic of movement. The simple change of venue as all-purpose vitamin and pepper-upper. Add to that a decadent English predilection for odd backwaters and you might be approaching some kind of raison d'être for what we were undertaking here.

S EEDINESS HAS a very deep appeal," Graham Greene wrote in his *Journey Without Maps.* He is a man with an eye for it, without question. "It seems to satisfy, temporarily, the sense of nostalgia for something lost; it seems to represent a stage further back." For lack of any better way to explain my own ongoing fascination with seediness, I'll go along with that. But in a world that is upgrading itself at an evermore dizzying rate, real seediness gets to be harder and harder to find. The city of Baltimore, where I used to work, had a delightfully seedy waterfront not too long ago. So did Boston. Now they both look the same: clean and prosperous. The details that once were seedy are now just quaint. You know how it goes.

To Americans, with our background of impermanence, the essence of seediness tends to be the decay of some past glory, achievement, or just glitter. A rusty Cadillac, for example. However, as Somerset Maugham, Joseph Conrad, and Greene himself knew well, there are places in the world that have been seedy from the start. A disproportionate number are port cities in the fever belt with maybe a revolution brewing up in the hills, and even they are becoming endangered institutions. The various fevers are mostly eradicated, sweat-stained linen suits have given way to shorts and Hawaiian shirts, rumors of El Dorado have become rumors of cheap beachfront acreage, and most of the revolutions have either already happened or are never going to. My research indicated that the last great fever ports left are to be found on the so-called Mosquito Shore of Central America, which stretches some 700 miles from Belize to Panama.

I was looking for stories that would be good enough to help me remember who I was. We were aiming to be the first American boat to sail the Caribbean coast of Nicaragua since the revolution. And at times it would be oddly comforting to remember that we were only the latest in a long line of gringos attracted here, like flies to flypaper . . . beginning with Columbus.

THE *DULCE* was a homebuilt launch docked at the end of the pier. The captain invited us to tie up next to him, helped us with our lines, and sent Richie the dock boy to fetch the immigration people. He was big, tough and friendly . . . and had a certain look about him.

"Born and raised in Key West, worked the lobster boats, went to Vietnam. I got back, everything was shot to hell. Faggots, tourists, and writers. Came here before I got into trouble." He built the *Dulce,* lives on her, makes money ferrying fishermen to and from Turneffe Lodge, a bonefishing paradise on an atoll out beyond the barrier reef.

I'd lived in Key West myself for a few years at the end of the seventies. I was working on a Vietnam novel. My two subteen daughters went to Key West public schools, wore their names in gold letters on chains around their necks and their hair like Farrah Fawcett. They snapped gum, hung out in the video parlor at the Searstown Mall, and swore in Spanish. I especially liked some of the Cuban Spanish they picked up.

My wife joined the astrologers in the mornings, the softball team (she was the pitcher and best hitter) in the afternoons, and the nickel-and-dime dope dealers in the evenings. Her life seemed to become very busy . . . too busy for me. Quite possibly I was just being a baby about it: After all, it was the seventies. I fell in love with somebody else, who seemed to have more time for me; soon my family had fallen to pieces. In a bar one night I looked up and saw a sign: YOU BETTER BELIZE IT.

"So you Belized it," I said to the captain.

He watched me, suddenly careful. "Never looked back."

We stopped in Key West on this trip. Looking back. A mistake, of course. The good edgy seediness was only left in the farthest back alleys and Duval Street was thick with tourists from the north. There was only one positive aspect that I could see: The astrologers, softball players, and nickel-and-dime dope dealers had all moved on.

I approached my old house on William Street with a sinking heart. My two daughters were now in college . . . my ex-wife was back in Boston with a solid, reliable man. Before I'd left ten years ago, I'd hidden two packets of Susan's love letters from Washington, D.C., way back under the eaves of the garage. I was sure they were still there . . . and they were, so far back I could only grasp them with the tips of my fingers. A little chewed by termites and smelling of mildew but intact. The owner of the house, a fashion consultant from New York, stood by with his mouth open.

We walked away from him into the nearby cemetery. Sitting on a sepulcher I opened one of the packets and began to read aloud at random. I was trying to be "lighthearted" about it. "If you're going to make fun of them, why don't you just burn them," Susan said before she left the cemetery. It was all downhill from there . . . on rainy days now we can smell the sweet mildew from the packets in the cubbyhole over the double bunk in the forepeak of the *Lord Jim*.

The few letters I had looked at after she left seemed . . . I have to say it . . . pretty goddamn pushy, from this juncture in history. *"What I've not told you directly (plenty of innuendo of course) is that at this moment and most of the time before now, I do want you to leave Holly and come with me . . ."* Well, she got her way. And I also have to admit that that "sweet urgency" (as we thought of it then) was one of the things I loved about her; and probably still is.

T HE OFFICIALS came down the pier in a body: the Immigration lady, the Customs man, the Port Captain and his girlfriend, and the Doctor. They climbed aboard and sat down in the cockpit. At least three races were in evidence. There was a festive air. The ship's entry papers to be filled out were printed in ornate black-letter script. "Do you have cold beer?" the Immigration lady said severely. "It's the custom, you know."

We did have beer: Bohemia from Mexico. Smooth and strong. Some of it was cold, more warm. The Immigration lady took hers to go (she didn't mind it warm) because she didn't drink on the job. "Do you mind if I check below?" the Customs man asked politely after his third cold Bohemia. The Port Captain's girl looked stunningly Mediterranean ... he was completely wrapped up in her. The Doctor never said a word. Our entry fee was ten dollars U.S. for the group's taxi fare to the pier. The Immigration lady gave us three months ... and a public relations packet of Belizean flag postcards to send home. In red on a blue field, a black man and a white man with axes and saws at the foot of a mahogany tree. The motto: *sub umbra florio.* "I flourish in the shade."

We were curious about the motto: where it came from, what it meant.

"There are many theories," said the Immigration lady briskly. "Probably all wrong."

Well ... and what about "Belize," the name of the country.

"That too, my friends. That too."

I T WAS Thanksgiving Day. After some prodding, the Doctor told us that the best and most nutritious dish in the country was Cowfoot Soup, available at a place called The Joker restaurant.

"Sounds interesting. How do you make it?"

"Take a goddamn cowfoot and bile it dahn, mahn. Put some lead in your pencil." The Port Captain's girl giggled and slapped him on the leg.

The pier was rocking as we trudged down the long perspective ... so was the deserted little park a few hundred feet up the shore. The park featured ankle-high crabgrass and a weathered stone obelisque to THOSE WHO GAVE THEIR LIVES IN THE GREAT WAR. Freshly played Chopin was coming from behind an enormous rose trellis on one of the wooden houses. We sat on the steps of the monument, listened until it was over, and when we got up again the park had stopped rocking. The palms and poincianas around the houses were full of enormous blue-black grackles, boat-tailed and white-eyed, that whistled at us in a possibly friendly way.

Down the side streets the old wooden buildings were ticking in the heat like barns. The first floors, their verandas and louvered shutters, were level with our eyes or higher . . . green latticework was around the pilings underneath. In a bare polished room through an open window a thin, severe lady with polished ebony skin, steel-rimmed glasses, hair in a bun, was carefully hanging ornaments on a huge Christmas tree.

The air was heavy with frangipani, oleander, and sewage. It got heavier and heavier. Then it started to rain. Hey-mahn-how-you-*been* type hustlers clustered under the broad overhang of buildings across from the market trying half-heartedly to sell us dope, and big, trussed sea turtles were sighing under the counters. A talkative retired sheriff from San Francisco who said he has been "in and out of here" for the last ten years warned us in particular about a hustler named Baby Brains.

There were two booths in the Joker Restaurant, one other customer (not eating), two women, and a baby. The Thanksgiving Day Parade in Philadelphia was on the television . . . we sat down in the empty booth and watched, fascinated. The rain splashed on the doorstep hypnotically. Time passed. Finally we asked about Cowfoot Soup.

"Oh, are you eating?" one of the women said in surprise. When she brought it, it was indeed rich, spicy, thick and delicious . . . you could almost feel it putting the lead into your pencil. In Filthydelphia, as we used to call it, the windchill factor was below zero and a huge, inflated Garfield the Cat was blown over on its side.

"That's where I'm from," I told the woman. "Philly. It's my hometown."

DURING THE disaster that had dogged me for the last couple of years, my father, my mother . . . *my forebears* . . . had come to be more and more important. I had a feeling they might save me if only I could find out more about them. So it seemed hopeful and fitting that for the first half of this trip at least we would be following in the footsteps of a distant relative who came through in 1839.

His name was Frederick Catherwood; he was the long-suffering yet obscure artist who accompanied explorer, diplomat, and author John Lloyd Stephens on his epic rediscovery of the Mayan ruins of Copán, Quiriguá, Palenque, Chichén Itzá, Tulum, Uxmal, and others. Frederick Catherwood illustrated the famous Stephens books *Incidents of Travel in Central America, Chiapas and Yucatan* (New York, Harper and Bros., 1841) with wonderfully dramatic sepia drawings, accurate down to the last hieroglyph, yet capturing all the mystery and wonder of his subjects' strange 900-year burial in the jungle. Still, when he died in an ocean liner disaster thirteen years later, all that appeared in the New York papers was a tardy item: "Mr. Catherwood also is missing." Other than the haunting drawings, no clue apparently survived as to what kind of man my relative really was.

Plain "Mr. Catherwood" or "Mr. C" is how he is referred to all through Stephens's book, as in:

> Mr. Catherwood was standing with his feet in the mud, and was drawing with his gloves on, to protect his hands from the moschetoes.

And:

Mr. Catherwood was thrown with such violence, that for a few moments, feeling the helplessness of our condition, I was horrorstruck.

And:

Mr. Catherwood's constitution was already severely shattered. Indeed, I became alarmed and considered it indispensable for him to leave the hacienda and if possible the country altogether.

Frederick Catherwood did have one biographer who published a short study in 1950. But facts were hard to come by, and what few facts there were did little to rescue my relative from the "ocean of oblivion," as Aldous Huxley put it in his introduction.

Not only had he failed to receive that public recognition to which his talents entitled him; he seemed also, in some sort, to have missed even private recognition. He was the friend and collaborator of painters and draftsmen; yet no likeness of him was ever made—or at any rate, none is now extant. He worked for many months with a vivid and copious writer, and he had met, in the course of his wandering life, many journalists in search of copy and many archeologists who shared his special interests; and yet none of them has left us an account of his personality or of the details of his private life. In spite of Mr. von Hagen's researches, the man whose strange and in many ways tragic career he has now reconstructed remains profoundly mysterious.

Tragic career indeed ... A beautiful, rich, well-connected woman was so taken with him as a young man she invited him to accompany her on an early expedition up the Nile. He would have been expedition artist and would have returned with some of Europe's first drawings of the pyramids, not to mention important backing and connections. But somehow he blew it with her before departure.

Twenty years later, he returned from Central America with a wonderful collection of carved Mayan lintels, sculptures, vases, and the like. He put them on exhibit in New York, along with enormous panoramic paintings (10,000 square feet apiece) he had previously done of Thebes and Jerusalem. The building burned down and everything was destroyed.

Still in his mid-forties, Catherwood gave up art, drafts-manship, and architecture (which he'd practiced in New York after the fire) for railroad engineering. He became involved pro-fessionally and financially in the construction of California's first railroad line, with the aim of establishing a new shipping port in San Francisco Bay and an attendant boom in land and commerce. Catherwood sailed to England to settle his affairs there. On his voyage back in September 1854 to reap the profits, the ship sank. "Mr. Catherwood also is missing."

"WE SHOULD do something about Frederick," my uncle said to me a while ago. "Why don't *you* write a book about him?"

"But there's nothing . . ."

"Don't let that bother you," my uncle said. I had just published my first novel.

"What?"

"What's the expression . . . 'Life imitates art?' "

I thought he was joking . . . good God . . . I didn't have time then anyway. But the idea stuck in my mind because, I'll have to admit, it seemed to be a way into a family that had always baffled me with its inscrutability; a way of finally coming to terms with where I came from.

Of course I myself have been accused of being inscrutable

... which is natural if you grow up in a household where the weightiest topic under public discussion is often the weather. On the other hand, I'm convinced there is such a thing as being *too* scrutable. If you tell everybody everything all the time ... what's left?

C LEANING OUT the attic of the family house near Philadelphia after my mother's death I made an interesting discovery. At the bottom of an old brassbound steamer trunk inscribed "D. Catherwood" (my grandfather) was a rosewood letter box filled with personal correspondence. I wasn't surprised that I'd never been told of it: My mother never told me anything about her family. She lived in her parents' house, but there were no pictures of them, no mementos. In true High Edwardian style, she had been consigned to an evil governess at an early age and never fully recovered. It was eerie to know that the bed in which she lay an invalid much of her later life was the same bed in which my grandmother had also been invalided. In both cases, the doctors were unable to diagnose the exact problem.

The letters, also in High Edwardian style, revealed almost nothing about the writers ... one or two might have been love letters, but it was hard to tell for sure. There was lots of news about the weather from my grandmother. In my mother's handwriting there was what seemed to be a page torn from a diary of her late teens. Watching her cousin's tennis lesson from the sidelines, she wrote:

> I would like to take some lessons too, and have suggested it, but they don't seem to take to the idea much so I don't insist. I guess they think I am not worthwhile, and they are right, although I *would* like to be able to do something *well,* no matter what it was, not be a little good for nothing and sit back and watch other people do things.

And there was a letter from New York, dated 1901, in an unfamiliar hand: *"Dear Cousin Daniel..."* It was from Mrs. Frederick Catherwood, who was then in her eighties and not feeling well. She wanted young Daniel, the closest living member of her late husband's family (the exact relationship has never been accurately established) to be in possession of certain facts. The letter ran to fifteen pages. Mrs. Catherwood's style was not High Edwardian. It was earthy and colloquial but her spelling and grammar were perfect.

Wildly excited, I rushed to my uncle's. Until then, almost nothing had been known about Catherwood's wife. She had been English, had borne him two sons (one in England and one in New York), and in November 1838 had lived at 466 Houston Street in New York City. That was it. What had happened to her and the two sons? Not even their names were known. Well, the answers were in this letter, along with some fairly telling psychological analysis of both Frederick Catherwood and his buddy John Lloyd Stephens.

How to be delicate about this? Some of the facts and analyses were rather compromising ... one would have liked to have heard their side of it, too. Still, what we had was all there was ... we owed it to posterity to use it, or at least release it. Didn't we? Whatever else you could say about it, it definitely made our mysterious, shadowy relative into a human being: Wasn't that exactly what we'd wanted?

My uncle disagreed. In the end, we decided not to release the letter. In fact, we destroyed it. Nothing more was said about my writing a book. The whole thing was so heated I forgot or suppressed most of what the letter had to say.

WHEN MY uncle himself died a few years later he left me his first edition of *Incidents of Travel.* The thick pages had the wonderful musty smell of old important knowledge. I was leafing through it for that smell and the illustrations, not really reading it, when I noticed a section had been underlined: "In regard to the stone hammock mentioned by Fuentes, and which, in fact, was our great inducement to visit these ruins, we made a special inquiry and search for it, but saw nothing of it."

Ah, yes. The stone hammock.

Francisco de Fuentes, in his eighteenth-century *Chronicles of the Kingdom of Guatemala*, describes the hammock as suspended between two pyramids near the Grand Circus of the Copán ruins in Honduras, (Stephens and Catherwood's first discovery). It contained two human figures, a man and a woman, appeared to be carved from a single stone, and "may be put in motion by the slightest impulse of the human hand."

My relative had found this hammock, his widow claimed. It hadn't been where Fuentes had described it; it was somewhere up in the hills around the ruins. She said Catherwood decided to keep the discovery to himself because at the time he and Stephens were "at odds" over a daughter of the owner of the finca where they were staying. He kept it to himself for years, waiting for a chance to go back and do something about it. Mrs. Catherwood only learned of the discovery herself going through his papers after his death.

Planning our own trip, we felt in a mood to give Mrs. Catherwood the benefit of the doubt at last. What the hell! Why not have a look for the hammock? If we didn't find it (this wouldn't be too surprising) we'd still have a good excuse to retrace Catherwood and Stephens's route through Belize, Guatemala, and Honduras to the ruins of Copán. In 150 years things would probably have changed, but sailors have always had a special appreciation for the fact that the more things change the more they remain the same.

S ETTING OUT in October 1839, they made an unlikely pair
... even more so than Susan (small, rounded, and fairly
scrutable for her size) and I.

Stephens, thirty-four, affected red Dundreary whiskers,
spats, pink frock coats, black cheroots. He was short, garrulous,
good-looking: a dandy. He loved the hullabaloo of early
nineteenth-century American politicking; he was well known in
Tammany Hall. Catherwood, thirty-nine, was big, quiet, and
unobtrusive . . . and that's about all we know about his appearance, even from his widow.

The fact that (according to that same widow) they were
both pathological womanizers made their association even more
unlikely. Before their trip to Central America, Stephens was
famous for having bought a sixteen-year-old Nubian girl's
clothing right off her back so that he could undress her in a public
market. Catherwood's dalliance with the famous *précieuse* Lady
Westmoreland had been the talk of the British expatriate set in
Rome. The question would have to be: how long could they
coexist "in the same valley."

Still, when the brig *Mary Ann* pulled into Belize Harbor
from New York in 1839, the two of them—bound for Copán and
its stone hammock—were the only passengers. Quite in line with
Mrs. Catherwood's subsequent revelations, Stephens's first observations were of the women:

> I could not help remarking that the frock was their only article
> of dress, and that it was the fashion of these sable ladies to
> drop this considerably from off the right shoulder, and to carry
> the skirt in the left hand, and to raise it to any height necessary
> for crossing puddles.

Womenwise, Belize is still the only Latin American country
where a foreigner can even talk to a respectable girl without

overtones of sin and macho taboo. A foreigner can in fact do more than talk. "No such thing as respectable women here, chum," a British soldier told us gaily.

Stephens was less enthusiastic to note (in spite of his Jeffersonianism) that this lack of inhibition went beyond sex to include class and race. *"Color was considered mere matter of taste."* It still does, directly because of the country's wonderfully seedy beginnings. Unlike the other British colonies—Jamaica, Barbados, etc.—no one there had any cause to lord it over anyone else. Thanks in large part to the hazards of its barrier reef, Belize has always been outside the mainstream of events even in Central America, a kind of apotheosis of marginalia. "If the world had any ends, British Honduras (as Belize was originally called) would surely be one of them," Aldous Huxley wrote in 1934, putting the echo to Stephens himself: "Belize was the last place made."

The Spanish, quick to colonize the interior, hated the place and after two or three explorations in the sixteenth century consigned it to the rubbish heap of history.

It was inherited by no-account British pirates and for 200 years or so, long after Spain had abdicated all responsibility, all Britain would officially say about it was "It is a settlement for certain purposes, in the possession and under the protection of His Majesty."

Jurisdictionally, it was unique in the Empire. Visitors from England wrote home about the "state of anarchy and confusion," and that the place was "an open receptacle for outlaws, felons, foreigners and all such men as fly from justice." Since all the place had to offer the Empire was mahogany and smuggled goods from the rest of Latin America, there was little economic incentive to regularize its position. In 1862, mostly one suspects out of embarrassment, they finally made it a full-fledged colony.

In the meantime local affairs were quite democratically run by public meeting, open to "numerous disreputable persons," according to British observers ... mostly freed slaves and mestizos (Spanish-Indians), of which there were more in Belize than in any other British possession. In 1814, when he arrived to assume the post of British Superintendant, Col. George Arthur wrote home that he was "astounded and dismayed by the prominent position of colored people in Society." However, when he left eight years later, he had decided they were the most stable element in the country. "I hardly knew whether to be shocked or amused at this condition of society," Stephens wrote when he and Catherwood came on the scene.

A FEW MONTHS before we arrived, George Price's party was reelected after a four-year hiatus and the seventy-one-year-old former seminarian reinstalled as Prime Minister. The peculiar essence of Belizean politics was never clearer: For twenty years under Price's quasi-socialist, paternalistic first administration the economy had stagnated to the point where it was entirely dependent on foreign aid. By all accounts, the new president, Esquivel, had turned things around. Things were brighter economically in Belize than ever before. But Esquivel rode in one limousine too many, with one too many well-dressed foreign dignitary. He didn't drive a beat-up Land Rover out into the smaller villages the way Price used to. He didn't have open house at his home on Sundays. He lost to a "Belize for Belizeans" platform . . . quite a shock to the United States. "They totally voted the man, not the issue," an amazed U.S. Embassy spokesman told us.

S IGN ON the prison door: PLEASE RING THE BELL ONLY ONCE. Sign in the street: IF YOU WANT YOUR CITY CLEAN THEN WHY DO YOU THROW GARBAGE?

Signs in the Belize Telephone Office:

1. THE BOOTHS ARE DESIGNED FOR NO MORE THAN TWO PER-SONS AT A TIME.

2. PLEASE REFRAIN FROM WRITING ON THE WALLS. THE BTO KEEPS THEM CLEAN AND ATTRACTIVE FOR YOUR CONVENIENCE.

3. PLEASE DO NOT PULL TELEPHONE RECEIVER OUT OF THE BOOTH.

4. PROPER ATTIRE SHOULD BE WORN. PLEASE KEEP YOUR SHIRT ON.

5. PLEASE DO NOT CONSUME ALCOHOLIC BEVERAGES NOR EAT ON THE PREMISES.

ALL NIGHT long the pier we were tied to would be full of Chinese from Hong Kong, fishing. Each family had paid some $20,000 for a Belizean passport. They were in the process of spending another $15,000 for illegal passage to the United States. Most had left China two or three years ago. Richie the dock boy didn't like them: They never paid any attention when he told them the dock was private property. In the morning, the *Lord Jim*'s rigging would be festooned with snagged hooks.

Richie was eighteen, worked out with weights and wanted to become a professional body builder. He weighed maybe 120 and had a way to go, but he was a serious hardworking kid . . . if only his life hadn't been ruined forever.

That happened when a 100-foot power yacht from Miami put into the dock. It was called the *Lucky Lady* . . . it had gold faucets in the bathrooms, Jacuzzis, a VCR in every stateroom, and much, much more. Richie, his eyes round as silver dollars, was adopted as a kind of mascot. For a week the ship and all its wonders belonged to him. Before they left the crew gave Richie a *Lucky Lady* T-shirt. That was a year ago. Now the T-shirt is faded and frayed and Richie has to wash it by hand to keep it from falling apart completely. When he showed us a picture of the *Lucky Lady* his hands were shaking. "They're coming back this winter," he said. "They're going to give me a job."

We didn't say anything.

"Sure, they'll be back," he said with a terrible kind of eager sadness. "Don't you think they'll be back?"

Richie liked to fool around with Marlene, a chambermaid at the hotel who was eight years older, had two babies, and treated him like a kid brother. Even in her white chambermaid's uniform Marlene's every movement had a slow, supple grace. Her large dark eyes were faraway, as if she were listening to distant music.

"What's there to do around here at night?" we asked her, watching her eyes become even more faraway.

"Well . . ." A wonderful, half-suppressed chuckle. "Thursday nights there's a live band at the Upstairs Cafe."

"But," Richie said quickly, "you probably wouldn't want to go."

"Why not?"

"Well . . . it's kind of rough. The Brits . . . they break things up, take off their clothes. They're not so nice."

I didn't tell them that my father is a "Brit"—and from a military family, too. My grandfather was with the 60th Rifles in India before the "Great War" . . . he could have been in Belize, although Belize was probably too seedy for the tony 60th. In my grandfather's day, at least, British regiments were run like clubs: The cachet of the 60th was always enviable although the only thing I personally got out of it was his old "Dominion grade" Holland & Holland double-barrel shotgun. "Dominion grade" was good for colonial use: It had no frills and could be replaced at minimum expense. Even so, I doubt whether the old blade ever took his clothes off in a bar. Or my father either: He once choked a drunken writer senseless . . . that's the only fight he ever told me about.

B RITISH TROOPS have been in Belize since 1786. A "joint service force" of 2,000 is there now, 8 years after independence, on a kind of open-ended billet against the "Guatemalan threat." It works out all right most of the time: Belize has no army of its own to speak of, and the Empire has shrunk to the point where the Brits have no other place to practice jungle training.

The troops are rotated through on a random basis for a six-month tour. The rank and file would rather be anyplace else . . . preferably rioting at a soccer game. There are admitted "community relations" problems, but they are caused mainly by men from "the Celtic fringes," according to Public Information Officer Capt. Guy Deacon, who sported a black eyepatch and an Etonian accent.

S USAN IS terrified of cows. She won't drive or even ride in a car going over sixty-five miles an hour. If you come quietly into a room where she is, she screams and jumps. Before this trip we had harbor-hopped (gunk-holed, as they say) a little in Maine and sailed a much smaller boat from Florida to Massachusetts but neither of us had done any real blue-water sailing or been outside well-traveled cruising areas.

We had owned the *Lord Jim* for only a year, barely enough to get to know her. Our slow, two-week passage from Fort Lauderdale to Belize had gone well, but that was the easy part. Now we were planning to go through tricky, unreliably charted stormy waters, into shallow inlets, open roadsteads, decrepit commercial wharves . . . the fever-port belt . . . places where "pleasure craft" never go.

Susan had no problem with it . . . quite the contrary. So I shouldn't have been surprised that she had no problem with the prospect of Thursday night at the Upstairs Cafe with Marlene and Richie and the Brits.

M ARLENE WAS dressed in a white sweater, black slacks, and flats. Her hair was up in a purple and gold bandanna. The whites of her eyes and her teeth were luminous. Richie looked a little abashed, as if he was already trying to distance himself from mishap. The Brits were packing the dance floor, still with their clothes on. The dance floor smelled of sweat and spilled beer and people were high-stepping around like nothing I'd ever seen since Small's Paradise in Harlem in the early sixties.

In the center of all this a black girl and a white girl were doing things I'd never seen done on a dance floor period. Their feet were the only part of them not moving. First they were back to front. Then back to back. Then front to front. One was bending backward, way way back, the other forward . . . hovering over the other held up by nothing but the beat. One of the Brits touched the white one, but withered in a blast from her eyes. Quite a distance from the dance floor, almost invisible in the shadows, a three man group was putting out sound. Punta, we were told later. It's called punta.

The Garifuna who developed punta are descendants of escaped British slaves from the Leeward Islands and the wild Carib Indians surviving at the time. In the late eighteenth century they were deported as troublemakers to the Bay Islands of Honduras. From there they settled along the mainland coast from northern Honduras to Belize. Now the Garifuna communities are tightly knit and prosperous, retaining their own language and their own music, their own celebrations, their own culture.

Punta sounds straight from West Africa. The rhythm is fast, driving, and complicated, the tune simple. You don't move your feet; it's all in the pelvis. Marlene was there in front of me with her hands above her head. Her dancing was subtle, languid, understated compared to the thrashing all around us. She barely seemed to move at all, but her *not* moving ornamented the beat in a heartbreaking way. Marlene built her own floating world around the beat, and gravely invited me to be part of it. For a minute or an hour I did become part of it.

Susan had been dancing with Richie, but at the end of the number a Brit with his back to me was deep in conversation with her: "Look, your fella's in love, you can *see* that. You'd better come away with me, my pet." Richie was hanging off to the side. Then, as if governed by an eccentric Central American deus ex machina, the band swung quickly into "I'm Dreaming of a White Christmas." We all shook hands. There it is: That's Belize.

It was pretty touching, actually. Walking home, the stars burned as brightly as if the temperature was twenty below zero and snow was crunching on the ground. The "Survival Series" of professional wrestling from Chicago—Hulk Hogan versus Crusher Casey—was visible on TV sets through all the windows, even in the fire station.

I CAME ON deck the next morning to see a new boat at the far end of the pier. She was flying the red and white dive flag and, oddly enough, I knew her name without having to read it off the transom . . .

On a blazing hot evening in June 1984, the dive boat *Gaviota* left Belize harbor with a party of eleven divers for a week on the reef. After they paired themselves up according to the buddy system, there were three left over: an elderly female chemistry professor from Pasadena State (born in Bulgaria and educated in Switzerland), a thirty-five-year-old male writer from Bridge-hampton (on assignment for *Esquire*), and a hollow-eyed psychologist from Boston in his early forties whose divorce trial was coming up a few days after the trip.

Linda, the twenty-seven-year-old Belizean divemaster, had a wonderful athletic body and a sunbeaten, weathered, outdoor face that tended to arouse sympathy. She was friendly, could free-dive to 100 feet, and didn't take any shit. The divers respected her and did pretty much what she told them to do . . . except for a nuclear physicist from Los Alamos, who was in a world of his own a lot of the time and could be quite intimidating. "You see that star over there?" he said one night to the magazine writer, who was trying to find out more about his work. "Well . . . we can just make that *disappear.*" Somehow he was able to use less air than everyone else and was always the last out of the water. His buddy loyally apologized for him: He was photographing nudibranchs—jewellike, rare little sea slugs that live in a close-focus tiny world about as far away from nuclear weapons as you could get.

The magazine writer had never seen a woman swim like Linda and was completely fascinated. Her face began to look strong and full of character instead of just beat-up. But the psychologist was completely fascinated too; he spent two or three evenings talking with her late into the night on the fantail and when, sometime around two A.M. with the Southern Cross peeking over the horizon, the smell of tarry Belizean marijuana began to curl from the fantail through the lower decks where the magazine writer lay reading, dozing, and listening, he knew it was a lost cause. And he tried to console himself with the thought that maybe, from the way he'd looked at the beginning of the trip, the psychologist was in greater need.

Early in the afternoon of the next fiery flat-calm day, with the *Gaviota* anchored on the dropoff near a laughably perfect "tropical isle" he watched the two of them swim back from the lagoon, a dive bag stuffed with conch hanging beneath them and their bodies touching from the shoulders to the knees. The psychologist's face, as he came out of the water, belonged to a new person.

He wanted to talk about it later and when he'd finished, strangely enough, the magazine writer felt as if it all had happened to *him*: "I didn't know a conch from a Great White Shark, but she wanted to go free diving for them so I followed along. She was swimming a little ahead of me leaving this trail of bubbles . . . I could feel every one of them. From her body to mine. We'd go through thermoclines where the water was so hot it distorted like heat waves, then icy cold. It was so calm the surface reflected her back so there was two of her. It was about fifty feet down, no problem for her. . . . you should have seen it: just soaring. She picked up the conch, never a wrong move, and floated back up toward me and I thought: my *God*, you know? I'm a *goner.*"

The late-night conversations on the fantail were about her childhood in Belize City. The psychologist listened (he said) less and less clinically, and finally the fate of his liberal, do-gooder's heart was sealed.

When she was seven, Linda's father, mother, two brothers, and sister moved from Redlands, California, into one of the grand old deep-verandaed bungalows on stilts in the fancy section near the American Embassy. Her father started a banana plantation downcoast, her mother—born in Mexico of Spanish parents—managed a clothing store. Linda and her brothers and sister went to St. Catherine's Academy to study under the Sisters of Mercy. Still in her school uniform one afternoon, she was raped on the front steps of the bungalow by a man who was so drunk he couldn't walk away afterward.

When Linda was twenty, the banana plantation went bankrupt. The buildings and equipment were looted and vandalized. Her father was finished with Belize; he decided to move the family to Charlotte, North Carolina, on what little money there was left. Linda said she was staying . . . after thirteen years she felt more Belizean than anything else. For a while, she rented a room in the old bungalow, but the new owner's attentions drove her out. She worked odd jobs for marginal tourist establishments in the cays until Tyll Sass, the owner, asked her to be assistant cook on the *Gaviota*. A couple of years later he offered to make her manager of his entire operation. So far she'd sidestepped.

"She wants to get married and settle down," the psychologist said. "My *God*."

"But does she want to leave Belize?"

"The hell with it. I can move here. Nothing to hold me up there anymore. And that same old bungalow she grew up in is for sale."

The magazine writer grinned and shook his head—it was all he could think of to do. Once again, it all could have been happening to him instead. But it wasn't.

The next day's diving was scheduled to be in the Blue Hole, a 400-foot-deep, 800-foot-wide shaft in the shallow lagoon of Lighthouse Reef. Eons ago, it was formed like a Florida sinkhole by the action of fresh water through limestone. Then the ocean rose and covered it. A good deal of the Blue Hole remained unexplored, but at diveable depths Cousteau and others had found grottoes with spectacular huge stalactites and stalagmites. There are legends of monsters and of tidal suction that can pull a diver down through the reef and spit him out somewhere inland.

The *Gaviota* dropped anchor on the lip at about eight A.M. Linda outlined the dive plan: They would proceed to the edge of the hole and check it out. She would descend first to the entrance of the grotto at 130 feet. The group would follow. After five minutes bottom time she would tap her tank three times with the blade of her knife, the signal to start up. "I don't want *anybody* going below me," she said. "And stay close. It's murky down there, easy to get separated." The psychologist, who usually dived with Linda, would buddy up with the magazine writer and the chemistry professor leaving Linda free to supervise.

The water inside the Blue Hole was actually black, with visibility about fifty feet. They sank quickly down the barren sides of the shaft toward Linda's strobe, and leveled off just short of 130 feet. Huge stalactites hung like church pillars from the mouth of the grotto. Strobes blinked in the gloom. It was out of this world.

The effect of nitrogen under pressure on the brain processes has been compared to one martini for the first 100 feet and another for each 30 feet thereafter. According to this measure, a person at 300 feet will have consumed 8; they had done 2. In fact, Rapture of the Deep (as nitrogen narcosis is romantically called) is quite different from drunkenness. There is an hallucinogenic dimension that at first makes colors and shapes extraordinarily vivid and new. A stronger hit can go either way: toward confidence and clarity or weirdness and paranoia. Finally come genuine hallucinations. Very narked divers have been known to give their mouthpieces to passing fish or simply to continue on down to whatever they see beckoning from below.

The hit was strong there. They'd descended quickly, and the scenery was unreal to begin with. The chemistry professor began taking photos at a tremendous rate, apparently losing track of where she was and bumping against the ceiling of the grotto. The sales manager of a big Cleveland chemical firm hung transfixed by what he saw in a square inch of stalactite. An accountant from Colorado disappeared upwards. The magazine writer stayed close to the picture-taking chemistry professor and when Linda tapped her tank he tapped her, hard. He'd lost track of the psychologist. What the hell, he thought in a drunken wave of resentment, *Linda will be looking out for him.*

He started up, beckoning frantically. The chemistry professor was following, but taking her sweet time. As they passed the 100-foot mark a cluster of strobes and shadows were visible above, Linda's was the only one left below.

His vision fogged as Linda's strobe divided into two . . . he shook his head to clear it, blinked, pressed his mask against his face. He was good and narked. He cursed the chemistry professor . . . what the hell was she trying to prove at her age?

The magazine writer felt an overpowering need for light and air. He turned his face to the surface and did not look back again until he was on the lip of the hole, in about fifteen feet of water. The chemistry professor was still rising slowly about forty feet farther down and somewhere below her two distinct strobes pulsed through the cloud of rising bubbles like the beating hearts of luminous deep-sea creatures.

The magazine writer (whose article was lost in some management reshuffle and never appeared) always stopped at this point in telling the story. It wasn't as if he was trying to keep his listeners in suspense . . .

"Well, *go on*," someone would say irritably.

NOTHING COULD be done, that was the horrible part. There were no roles for heroes. None of the divers could go back down with spare tanks without skewing their decompression tables off the charts and risking the bends—in which a too-sudden release of pressure causes the blood literally to boil with crippling nitrogen bubbles. The captain and crew of the *Gaviota* weren't divers themselves. There was no launch to position over the bubbles so that the spare tanks could be lowered from the surface. And ultimately it was questionable whether spare tanks would have done anything but prolong the agony. The psychologist was twenty feet below Linda before she noticed him and going down pretty fast. She might have caught him at 200, but by then he would have been narked silly—a dead weight, or worse: He might have struggled. The water had cleared up down there so she could see his strobe recede into the distance, recede and recede until it became a tiny pinprick in the black, but never disappear. His bubbles continued to rise in regular clusters like silver grapes.

The magazine writer was waiting for her at fifteen feet. He still had plenty of air and offered his mouthpiece so she could buddy-breathe to decompress. She needed to hold there for at least five minutes to be safe but she swam slowly past him. They reached the dive platform on the stern of the *Gaviota* together. José the deckhand climbed down to help with the gear, the other divers watched from the stern. Nobody said a word.

Linda climbed up the swim ladder onto the dive platform and sat there, her head down, her hands clasped between her thighs. José stood uncertainly by. The magazine writer was frozen on the swim ladder, still half in the water. The young captain, John, came down and put his hand on her shoulder. "What happened?"

She shook her head. He took his hand off her shoulder. "What happened?" he asked the magazine writer.

"I didn't see. Somehow he got below her."

"He was looking out for me," the chemistry professor explained. "I was out of my mind taking pictures."

The young captain looked up at the divers. "Nobody saw?"

Some of the divers looked at Linda. Some looked at each other. Some looked at the surface of the water in the Blue Hole, where the psychologist's bubbles could still be seen.

After a while, the bubbles dwindled to a thin stream and then stopped. Linda didn't move. The magazine writer thought he had better leave her alone and climbed up into the boat. The young captain was already on the radio to Belize Services. "We lost a man in the Blue Hole," the divers could hear him saying. He gave the psychologist's name and spelled it out in U.S. military style. "Yeah, of course . . . we're coming right back in."

"Hey John," the nuclear physicist said when the captain

had signed off and come back out of the wheelhouse. "We got two days left."

The young captain's mouth opened as if he were about to say something, but he didn't.

"We paid for a seven-day trip, John. We've only been out for five."

The nuclear physicist was calm and matter-of-fact. He could have been talking about the weather. His expression—a grin with one side of his mouth—was the expression he had when he came up from a dive.

The magazine writer felt the blood pulsing behind his eyes. "You asshole," he said to the nuclear physicist. "Why don't you go peddle your bombs."

The other divers began to make small insignificant movements, as if testing their ability to move at all. The chemistry professor patted her hair; the Colorado accountant crossed his arms; the chemical sales manager scratched his neck; a young woman intern from Chicago wiped her eyes and sniffled. The nuclear physicist was looking down at Linda in his calm undersea way.

"Wow." The accountant shook his head.

The captain started the *Gaviota*'s engine. Then he turned it off again and came out of the wheelhouse. "If you people want to finish the trip, we'll finish the trip." His voice sounded very young.

"You have to be kidding," the magazine writer said.

"Nothing like this has ever happened to me before," the captain said. "I'm kind of at a loss."

"I think everybody would like to get off this boat as quickly as possible," the magazine writer said. The captain's mouth opened and closed again. He shrugged and raised his hands. "Everybody except Doctor Strangelove," the magazine writer said.

There was a sound from the dive platform. In a second, they could see Linda doing a swift graceful crawl away from the *Gaviota* and the Blue Hole across the pale shallow water of the lagoon.

"Shit . . ." the chemical sales manager ripped off his jersey and began to undo his pants.

"You'll never catch her," the young intern's boyfriend said. "Not a chance."

"But she'll come back," the chemistry professor said. "Just a swim, of course."

"You happy?" the other Colorado accountant said to the nuclear physicist, who just raised his eyebrows.

The captain started the engine of the *Gaviota* and yelled at José to get the anchor up. In not too long a time the boat was under way across the vast pale lagoon. A big thunderhead rising over the mainland twenty miles away reflected in the smooth surface. The divers gathered on the bow, even though by this time Linda was only visible from the bridge with field glasses.

She climbed back on board quietly when the boat came alongside her and went down to her cabin. Someone called for a show of hands on continuing the trip. One by one they rose until it was unanimous. Yes, they'd go on. The magazine writer's hand was not among the first, but it wasn't last either.

A few years later, when the magazine writer returned to Belize on a book project, Tyll Sass told him that Linda was still working as divemaster on another boat. She never did get married and settle down. The magazine writer wondered if chance would have it that he would run into her, but chance did not. Or if it did, he didn't recognize her; light-skinned women age fast in the tropics. Still, he would always remember the way she had looked underwater that day diving for conch . . . and he had never even seen her.

I T WAS a still, white-hot afternoon and the grackles could be heard whistling all over town. We were discussing the whereabouts of Tropical Storm Karen with our neighbor on the pier,

Tyll Sass, owner of the dive boat *Gaviota*, who was about the closest one could come in Belize to a resident expert.

Tyll smiled over our shoulders and waved. A tall, auburn-haired woman in tiger-stripe camouflage fatigues rode up on a Yamaha 750 motorcycle. The motorcycle was painted with jaguar spots. She parked it at the foot of the pier and walked toward us with long, swinging strides. "Hey Tyll! Know anything about Caterpillars?"

The generator at the zoo was acting up.

The Belize Zoo . . . imagine it! It is not, as you might have thought, a collection of local oddballs and eccentrics. Certainly the director, Sharon Matola, thirty-five, formerly of Baltimore, has been known to arrive at parties sporting a boa constrictor on her neck. But still, Belize has always been the kind of country where such behavior occasions only a catty remark. *"She doesn't have to use the animals to make herself exotic, does she?"*

No she doesn't. At an early age, Sharon decided that her middle-class Catholic girlhood in suburban Baltimore had gone far enough. She joined the Air Force. Soon she was doing jungle survival training in Panama. "I was the only woman in a class of sixteen. I couldn't believe what chimps those guys were. I couldn't believe they wouldn't do things like eat iguana after no food for seven days." In not too long a time she was the first female instructor at the survival school, discovering that "in some areas I could be good."

After four years she was back in civilian life, a college student with Uncle Sam paying the bills. First it was Russian at the University of Iowa ("A man was involved"), then biology at the New College of Sarasota. She was working part time at the Mote Marine Laboratory with Eugenie Clark, the shark expert, but was not impressed. "That woman was so rude to me . . . she ignores other women, concentrates completely on men. I decided that if I ever get anywhere in this world that's the way I will not be."

The laboratory was impressed enough with Sharon to send her down to Belize one summer on a reef study. She was particularly fascinated by one set of statistics that had nothing to do with reefs: Belize has the lowest density of human beings of any country in Central America and the highest density of jaguars in the world.

Sharon was doing graduate work on tropical fungi at the University of South Florida in Tampa when she saw an ad in the *Herald Tribune* of Sarasota, circus headquarters to the hemisphere. A big Mexican circus, The Holiday International, needed women dancers. Perfect! She could dance at night and collect mushrooms during the day. Six girls answered the ad. They were flown to Guadalajara but then five girls were flown back. "Said they weren't what they were looking for." What happened to the dance act is unclear, but Sharon herself was offered a job doing the lion act with a family-run spin-off, the Suarez Brothers, touring the smaller towns for seven months.

For Sharon, it was a piece of cake. "The cats were already trained. All you had to do was crack the whip a little, get them to respect you. Anybody could do it. You just can't be afraid." There were six tigers, four lions. No problem. The Mexican men were something else. No, she never went so far as to sleep *in* the cages with her animals to get away, but she did sleep on top of them routinely. Men carrying guitars and bottles of tequila would serenade her from down below and the cats would roar.

Back in Tampa after the tour, Sharon got a letter from a man she'd never met. A round-trip ticket to Belize was enclosed. A British wildlife filmmaker named Richard Foster needed someone to take care of his animals between films. Mutual friends had told him about her . . . if she didn't like the setup she could go right back.

She liked the setup a lot, but after a while Foster found he couldn't afford to maintain the twenty animals anymore. He told Sharon they'd have to go. But Sharon thought that to release back into the wild animals that were "accustomed to being around people, film stars in their own right, and used to daily care to the point of being pampered," was out of the question. Still, somehow they had to be paid for. Maybe the answer was a little zoo.

"Anyone hearing my plan only had this to say, 'you're crazy.' I listened carefully to their logic. 'Belize is a poor country, and it doesn't have the population to support a zoo. Why, more people live in a square mile of Manhattan than this entire country!' I continued to listen. 'And look at that road—it would take someone over an hour to drive to the zoo from the nearest town. And to see what? A few animals in cages? It will never work.' . . . With that encouragement a zoo was born."

She found that Belizeans were fascinated by their wildlife and almost totally ignorant about it. Most of them lived in towns and feared the bush. They thought the tapir would skin them alive with its flexible nose. Meanwhile, in most of Central America, wildlife populations were being decimated by development of one kind or another. Belize was the least developed but the process seemed to be only a matter of time.

"The purpose of a little zoo became clear. How could anyone expect someone to want to protect something they did not understand or know?"

T HAT WAS six years ago. There have been some changes. April the Tapir, roaming around loose, never skinned anyone alive with her flexible nose but she did get so big it hurt a lot when she stepped on toes, and sometimes she went through floors. Now she has a pen. There are seventy other local Belizean animals instead of twenty. Five hundred kids a month are bussed out from school in a city-sponsored education program to be shown around by the fourteen-man Belizean staff. Prince Philip and Princess Anne have also visited. And 1,000 acres across the road have been donated for an expanded facility. Sharon says she has already raised $100,000 for it and the rest will be paid for through the offices of Gerald Durrell . . . who wrote the books she grew up on: *A Zoo in My Luggage, My Family and Other Animals,* etc. A master plan has been donated by Jones and Jones, in Seattle, the architectural firm that has designed similar plans and "natural habitat exhibits" for the San Diego Zoo, the Honolulu Zoo, and others.

We followed Sharon around her zoo. The animals were living under their Belizean names:

Mountain cow—tapir
Night walker—kinkajou
Bush dog—ferret
Jungle rabbit—agouti
Bamboo chicken—iguana
Snake waiting boy—lizard
Wowla—boa constrictor
Quash—coatimundi
Gibnut—paca

Hand-lettered signs spoke for them:

I am a Great Black Hawk—but guys who take shots at me are Great Big Turkeys. You know, we get shot at because people think we go after their chickens for their dinner. CHICKEN? No Boy!! We Great Black Hawks like to eat insects and snakes. So please tell your friends—Great Black Hawks eat Snakes. Please—let us have a future in the wild.

When Sharon was about twenty feet away from one of the cages we began to hear a noise like the proverbial small engine. It was Inca, the puma. Sharon put her fingers through the wire and Inca scratched herself against them as if they were magic fingers. Purring now like a Porsche 911, Inca leapt to a runway level with Sharon's head. Sharon opened a door at the end of the runway, Inca put her head out, they touched noses and rubbed cheeks.

"The cat certainly seems to like you."

"Yes, she does."

"Actually, she loves you, doesn't she?"

Sharon just smiled.

"But how did you . . . ?"

Her long strong brown face split in a grin. "Professional secret, buddy." The cat was in heat, it turned out, and had learned where to find relief. Sharon was somewhat different from your run-of-the-mill expat, but, as we were coming to understand, Belize is also a country where, as Nabokov wrote about great literature, "you do not encounter mere traditional notions which may be borrowed from the circulating library of public truths, but a series of unique surprises . . ."

A T SIX A.M. pea-soup fog covered the face of the water around us with a chilling damp, making us feel as if we were in Maine. Or going crazy. Something was up. Fishing smacks and sand lighters ghosted by on their way out of the harbor and you could hear every word that was said on board . . . they were talking about Tropical Storm Karen.

Karen had been headed back out to sea last night: no problem. But aboard the *Gaviota*, Tyll Sass had the latest: Karen had done a 180 and now the entire Belizean coast was on storm alert. Winds in the storm center were over fifty miles an hour. The outer edge was due about noon.

It's times like these that make you wish you were doing your traveling by muleback, backpack, railroad . . . the freedom, the freedom. A boat ties the traveler down, defines him or her whether he or she wants it or not, and sometimes suffocates him (or her) with the heavy weight of material responsibility or beyond that just plain fear. The fear of losing the boat is sometimes worse than the fear of drowning, sometimes not as bad. Depends on how romantic you're feeling at the time.

The trade-off is that a boat provides its own unique viewpoint on the world. When I was working as a correspondent in Vietnam just after Tet in 1968 I knew an Australian construction worker who lived on a sailboat docked in the Saigon River. He'd watch the ships arriving with green troops and leaving with . . . well . . . men who had spent a year or more in a manner now well-known to us. Weeping Vietnamese girls holding their babies and waving good-bye. He would be offered huge sums of money to smuggle all kinds of things. For sport he would invite people waterskiing up the river. He'd have dinner by the light of illumination rounds hanging over the huge swamp (said to be full of VC) on the other side of the river and talk about the odds of an attack. Every day brought its piece of dock scuttlebutt to be stored away. Schemes and dreams. He told me he was going to write a book about it all and I've always envied him that book even though as far as I know he never wrote it.

Hilaire Belloc, the protofascist British essayist, novelist, and politician, used a boat somewhat in this manner (not so much as a vehicle of transportation as of a certain type of understanding) and wrote in the twenties: "There is in this aspect of land from the sea I know not what of continual discovery and adventure, and therefore of youth, or, if you prefer a more mystical term, of resurrection."

Resurrection, indeed. Politics aside, it sounded good. And it was true about landfalls, what he said.

I really had no choice, though. Boats are what my father taught me about . . . my father, the classic black sheep, who did not follow his father and brothers into an honorable military life but instead sailed away across the Atlantic in a leaky old yawl called the *Pansy* with two ragtag buddies . . . one of whom wrote a book about it all, called *Going Native.*

My father is described this way:

He is pretty well the perfect Englander. Over six feet, thirty years old; I was first impressed, before having met him, by a little tale about him. It went this way. A doctor once met his mother, reputed to be very beautiful and, not knowing her, tried to make his best conversation and most suitable small-talk. It so happened that his talk took the turn of describing a certain young man who, in his considered professional opinion, was the most perfect physical specimen that had ever come under his notice. It was only after the doctor had gone on for some time and forgotten himself enough to be actually eloquent, that Charles' mother admitted to the startled doctor that she was his mother.

But Charles himself is very slow-going, very English. Nevertheless, I've kept on noticing that he is always very quickly on the spot when anything definite enough has to be decided or done. He gets there in one, though with a lazy, almost stupidly elegant and drawling fashion. . . .

My father taught me to love and understand boats, although until now I'd never had a real chance to test the knowledge. I inherited at least half his body: his arms and legs; the middle part is more cylindrical than wedge-shaped. And the face that made my mother spurn her eligible Philadelphia suitors might also have lost a little in translation. But I have no complaints . . . "I have never been mugged," as writer Jim Harrison likes to say.

He had a harder time with directions and destinations . . . and the reason for that, I do believe, was that after he married the crucial task of navigation passed out of his hands. My mother laid the course from then on, although he still got to steer. What he passed on then to us kids was just generalized paralysis in the face of all authority . . . an excellent reason for a sailing trip where there are two cocaptains and no crew.

It's too late for him now. He has a pacemaker, an artificial hip, and two Ronald Reagan hearing aids that do absolutely no good. But I did want to show him, before he dies, that the lessons took.

S TORM BULLETINS were coming in now about every half hour on Radio Belize and a rising east wind was shredding the fog and our nerves. Tyll Sass was going to keep the *Gaviota* at the dock—she was heavy, rough, and well-enough moored for it—but counseled departure for us. "Better get sailing. How long have you been here anyway . . . a week and a half?" He grinned reassuringly. He knew a hurricane hole in the mangroves on the Drowned Cays where he thought we would be snug enough. Richie cast us off with that same sad eagerness—*"When are you coming back?"*—and we headed out into the whitecaps, our Belizean courtesy flag snapping and crackling from the spreader.

There is nothing as snug as a good hurricane hole with a storm approaching. As Tyll had said (did we ever doubt him?) this one was really good: The creek was deep but not too deep, wide enough for us to swing but narrow enough for perfect protection from all sides, the bottom soft mud and wonderful holding. The mangroves tossed against the gray sky, the wind whistled around the deckhouse, the *Lord Jim* veered and hunted on the anchor rode and the little two-inch waves gurgled cozily against the thick fiberglass of her hull.

We watched a manatee rolling down the creek's corrugated surface and hoped the storm was going to be really bad. The wind seemed to be getting stronger. Didn't it? We took off our clothes, got under the covers, and held each other tight. When Tropical Storm Karen perversely veered back out to sea we were disappointed, but we'd had a pretty good time anyway. Susan told me about when she'd been stopped at a light in a bad part of Washington, D.C., and a guy had opened the passenger-side door and gotten in with her. "Don't scream. I'm not going to hurt you. Just drive." She did scream, pulled her feet off the pedals, kicked him back out the door into the street, took off. She drove hard out of the area and pulled into the parking lot of a supermarket. Sitting there, shaking so hard she couldn't turn the engine off, she felt her body surrender to a grinding orgasm.

Susan comes from one of those New England families in which insanity is passed down along with the Chippendale and the pewter and the Harvard education. She has the awesome nose, the determined chin, the thin straight lips, the steady eyes, the overall cachet of Yankee respectability which in that odd part of the world always signal defective genes.

Susan wasn't the one to get it in her generation . . . that honor, or duty, fell to her twin brother. It would not be fair or accurate to say that the other four kids all breathed sighs of relief, and yet the system did seem one of primogeniture. Her brother accepted it in fairly good spirits, kicking his heels up and taking his clothes off in public places because he could no longer be held responsible. The others all circled the wagons, maintain close contact with each other, and live lives with very well-defined borders. Susan had to call them every week on the single-side-band and for those few minutes the *Lord Jim* eerily became a suburb of Boston.

It's different in my family. We're all a little strange, and quite a bit of it comes from having no sense of borders at all. Things tend to be fogbound, undifferentiated . . . inscrutable. Susan shows me the edges.

I CAN STILL hear my ex-wife's lawyer in divorce court:
"And how did you leave your wife and children . . . Gordon? What physical means of transportation did you choose?"
"A boat."

"What kind of a boat?"

"A sailboat."

"You mean . . . Gordon . . . you just . . . *sailed away?*"

Indeed. And my fortyish sister spends a lot of her time training for the Ironman Triathlon in Hawaii: 2 miles of ocean swimming, 100 miles of bicycling, 26 miles of running—the world's most demanding athletic event. She's been in two already.

Incidentally, my ex-wife ended up with the little boat I sailed away in . . . it turned out to be registered in her name. She had it hauled out of the water and never got around to putting it back in.

N EXT DAY we rode the remnants of Karen south, in protected water behind the barrier reef. The wind was on the stern quarter out of the northwest at about twenty-five knots . . . we boomed along at top speed (eight knots) and the Maya Mountains grew clearer and clearer out of the flat coastal plain. Andy Palacio was singing his punta hit "Bikini Panty" over Radio Belize and to the east, between us and the reef, lay an improbably picturesque archipelago of palm-tree islets.

L IKE MANY Americans who grew up cherishing our inalienable right to litter, it's been hard for me to get used to the fact that any modern appreciation of nature and its wonders has to deal first and foremost with the issue of man's destruction of them. Peter Matthiessen, who wrote in 1959 a comprehensive history of man's effect on North American wildlife, was among the first:

Today's voyager, approaching our shores through the oiled waters of the coast, is greeted by smoke and the glint of industry on our fouled seaboard, and an inland prospect of second growth, scarred landscapes, and sterile, often stinking rivers of pollution and raw mud, the whole bedecked with billboards, neon lights, and other decorative evidence of man's triumph over chaos . . .

One way to deal with the problem has traditionally been to leave the polluted, fouled United States to malcontents like Mattiessen and travel to the wild frontier of the Third World. Belize, for example, which conservationists hail as being one of the most environmentally intact places in the hemisphere:

The Belizean barrier reef is the second largest in the world and the greatest manifestation of the coral reef ecosystem in the Western Hemisphere for its size, unique array of reef types and luxuriance of corals thriving in such a pristine condition . . . It is practically all that is left of a flourishing and nearly pristine reef environment in the Caribbean. (From a 1983 study commissioned by the New York Zoological Society)

The system includes most of the Atlantic's few atolls. You can land on islets that have quite possibly never been landed on before. You can sail for days without seeing another human being. If you dive in some of the passes, as we did, you're likely to find yourself surrounded by schools of six-foot tarpon as thickly packed as minnows. The silver-dollar-scaled creatures actually resemble huge minnows, creating the perception that one has shrunk to a fraction of one's normal size.

The extent of the huge reef system, in fact, produces the same healthy feeling of insignificance in the traveler. There seems to be no way that man can ever make a difference. Even now, seven years after the study was completed, according to New York Zoological Society Caribbean conservation director Archie Carr, III, "The reef is in remarkably good shape."

You have to keep sailing, as we did, down the rest of the Caribbean coast to really understand how strange, unique, and wonderful this condition is. You have to sail into a few of the sterile, depopulated lagoons in Guatemala, Honduras, Nicaragua; dive on some of the barren reefs. Then you have to wonder, with Carr, Matola, Matthiessen, and the rest, how in God's name can Belize hold out. And if there is anything at all we can do to help.

TOURIST WEATHER. We drifted pleasantly down inside the reef, stopping at various deserted islets, diving for fish and lobster, watching the coastline rise and, as John Lloyd Stephens wrote offhandedly from the deck of his steamship, *"assume an appearance of beauty and grandeur that realized my ideas of tropical regions."*

The protecting reef to the east of us straggled to an end and we began to feel the touch of the trade wind swells: We were now in the Gulf of Honduras, that corner of the Caribbean common to three of the six countries on our itinerary: Belize, Guatemala, and Honduras. The other three (Nicaragua, Costa Rica, and Panama) are around the remote corner of Cape Gracias a Dios, more than 300 miles due east against the wind.

THE SERIOUS mountains of Guatemala, three times as high as anything in Belize, loomed out of the haze to the south. To the west, a row of low bumps must have been the famous Seven Hills of Punta Gorda ... landmark to conquistadores, buccaneers, and modern-day contrabandistas. Punta Gorda is the southernmost outpost in Belize ... remoteness piled on remoteness. A forest of radio towers topped by strobe lights showed where the Voice of America spoke sense to the convoluted, Latinate problems of the rest of Central America.

Hart and Stone's encyclopedic *Cruising Guide to the Caribbean and the Bahamas* recommended a little mangrove island a few miles west called Frenchman's Cay as a good place to spend the night. Hart (or Stone) stopped there fourteen years earlier . . . at the time, it was owned by an ex-Navy American named Dick More. More had "passed on" but his house was "surrounded by lush tropical plants, coconut palms, and livestock, including a 1,000 pound hog." There was a stone pier and a protected deepwater anchorage . . . it sounded good. Maybe More had returned . . . he would be worth meeting, to live way out here.

We had no trouble finding a configuration of islands that conformed to the chart's positioning of Frenchman's Cay but something was off: There was no stone pier. We looked north and south through the green channels and up the creeks. Nothing else came close. We returned, anchored and scanned the mangrove shore with field glasses. No house was visible, but there were some palm trees and a few stones that could have been a pier a long time ago. We had only one hour of daylight left.

WE ROWED ashore in a flat gray calm with the Voice of America strobes pulsing in the distance. The mangrove noises were too loud in the quiet: pop of snapping shrimp, rustle of fiddler and hermit crabs, croak and thrash of cormorants, herons, and egrets, whine of insects, yelp of kingfisher. A big seagrape tree with round platterlike leaves stretched over the ruins of the pier, if they were in fact ruins . . . we rowed under it and pulled the dinghy up onto a dark little beach.

The ground was damp and muddy, only a few inches above sea level and full of tiny crab holes. What might have been a trail led away from the stones and the sea grape toward a big mango. But it might just have been an open area in the scrub.

Anyway we followed it. It was too quiet to talk. Our skin was beginning to prickle and smart with no-see-um bites. And the sucking, squishing noises of our own passage mingled with the rest of the unnaturally loud sounds on Frenchman's Cay.

The land rose a few inches and became sandy. We began to see land-crab holes that seemed enormous in the failing light . . . big enough for crabs the size of dogs. At the mouth of each hole the crabs had shoveled out mountains of dirt. The tracks of their legs led in and around the area and had us checking over our shoulders in case one was steamrollering up behind us.

Choking in the scrub were a few hibiscus bushes and banana trees. There was an algae-discolored cement cistern, half filled with leaves, branches, and coconut rinds. On the perimeter of the sandy high ground was a pile of bottles, some of which looked old enough to be worth money.

Susan wanted to get out of there, I wanted to go on: That's the way it usually is. And as usual, we compromised by going on "just a little bit farther." I wanted to find the house.

The trail led from the big mango tree to the grove of palms. Long rank grass rustled against our legs . . . above us hung threateningly large clusters of heavy ripe coconuts, bringing to mind a story I knew about Charles Lindbergh (who, incidentally, landed the first airplane in Belize in 1927).

Lindbergh was invited to lunch on a private island near Nassau in the Bahamas. The lavish lunch was laid out on picnic tables in a seaside coconut grove: Alsatian wine, barbecued pig, fresh-caught fish, natives strumming on guitars, etc. Lindbergh would have none of it, at least not until they moved the lunch indoors. He had carefully assessed the odds of a coconut falling on his head and didn't like them. We kept on the perimeter of this grove in case Lindbergh was right. Why take unnecessary chances?

The high ground receded into mud. Ten-foot-high mounds of moss-covered stones were visible on the other side of a muddy glade—heaped there by a hurricane, apparently. There was a flash of something brown moving among the stones. We kept to the high ground.

We never found the house or any trace of it, but a little to one side of the palm grove we came across a pole lean-to thatched with palm fronds and floored with banana leaves. In front of the lean-to was a pile of enormous red land-crab shells and a couple of bottles. Even in the failing light the shells looked fairly fresh. Now we could feel eyes on us. And we both agreed that it was definitely time to leave.

At least our dinghy was where we'd left it. Back on the *Lord Jim* we unlimbered the 12-gauge Browning automatic and loaded it with three-inch express shells of triple-ought buckshot. The eyes were still there. The sun was well down, but the sky had cleared up and was full of starlight. We sat on the foredeck listening to the noises, watching the strobes pulse and the mountains loom and wondering if there was any stranger place in the world. We were more than a month out of Fort Lauderdale and the trip seemed to be truly under way.

T HE STORY of Frenchman's Cay was easy to come by in Punta Gorda . . . it was in fact only one of many you could come by there, ranging from the story of the doomed Toledo Settlement begun by ex-slaveowners from the post–Civil War South to rumors of lost gold mines up in the unexplored reaches of the Maya Mountains. Punta Gorda is Belize's own end of the line, and the fact that the ancient green schooner we anchored next to in the harbor was inhabited by a pair of New York artists was only as exotic as everything else.

The ever-rakish John Lloyd Stephens, passing through here

with Frederick Catherwood on the Belize City–Guatemala steam packet, tells a curious story of his own about Punta Gorda. At a local baptism, it seems, the beautiful young mother suddenly thrust her baby into his arms. Stephens never explains why. He does admit that he stopped the ceremony and tried to avoid taking the baby but the woman was persistent. Apparently the baby ended up with Stephens's name. "I can only hope that in due season it will multiply the name and make it respectable among the Caribs," Stephens concluded mysteriously. Catherwood's feelings and comments on the incident went unrecorded, as usual.

Dick More first came to Belize after World War II and a stint with the Navy's Underwater Demolition Teams mining harbors in France. He was a big, beefy man whose gunmetal scalp shone through his crewcut, square widely spaced teeth like piano keys, fists as hairy, hard, and brown as coconuts . . . he fit right in. First he ran dive trips on the reef, operating out of an old wooden hotel next to the post office at the foot of swing bridge over the Belize River. Dick had a lot of friends, they had a fine time, the hotel burned down . . . not necessarily in that order. Dick drifted south and made landfall on Frenchman's Cay: It was love at first sight, if you can believe that.

On Frenchman's Cay he built a palm-thatched bungalow without walls and sent out the word: His friends were welcome—not just welcome, *expected.* His friends were all like him. They brought a live suckling pig to roast in a luau, but as the evening progressed the pig got harder and harder to catch. In the morning it was still alive and growing rapidly.

Dick took to island life. He lived in a pair of olive-drab Navy skivvies and hung plastic fruit from his newly planted fruit trees. To bathe in he had an old bathtub that had somehow floated ashore on the island. To keep off the no-see-ums he had an ongoing fire of coconut husks (the column of white smoke towering from the palms became a landmark to Punta Gordans.) For

medicine he had Belize's own Charcoal Rum, at $1.50 U.S. a
fifth. And to drink it with, when his friends were away, he had a
spider monkey whom people from Punta Gorda remember as
"very nasty." Finally there was the pig, which now weighed
1,000 pounds, and which even Dick More treated with respect.
At least he didn't talk of eating it anymore, but sometimes vice
versa. As time went by he found himself feeling seedier and
seedier, but never to the point of following his friends' advice and
leaving the island. Why not?

One day Dick More's friends came to Frenchman's Cay and
found him dead. Liver failure. The pig hadn't got him: He had
died in the bungalow and the stairs wouldn't support the pig; it
had broken them trying to get up. The first thing Dick More's
friends did was to shoot it.

In more mordant moments he had told them how he wanted
to be laid to rest: a proper military burial, wrapped in the United
States flag with a twenty-one-gun salute. They complied. His
grave was to be in the big ten-foot-high rock piles we had seen:
ancient Mayan burial mounds, it turns out. The idea was to bring
confusion on any archaeologists who might happen to excavate.
So he was still there. The flash of brown we had seen was an
eight-foot, very poisonous viper called a fer-de-lance that people
in Punta Gorda think of as a kind of honor guard.

After the burial, his friends butchered the pig. They ate
some of it in memory of their friend. Four *pangas* were needed to
carry the rest back to Punta Gorda.

B EFORE WE left Belize we had the New York artists on the
old green schooner over for a drink. They were waiting for a
favorable breeze to wherever. We watched the sun set behind the
jungle-thatched mountains behind the town and then the talk
came around to Dick More and his island.

"But why didn't he leave?"

"Maybe he ran out of time," the girl said. She herself was thin and fast moving, very New York. "The sun goes down *really quickly* here. Haven't you noticed? You wake up, you have breakfast . . . then it's dark."

Two

Guatemala

AILING FROM one country to the next on the Caribbean coast of Central America doesn't make as much difference as you'd expect. Most of the greater Mosquito Shore from Belize to Panama grew up the same way: jurisdictionally part of the Spanish Main but under the de facto control of ragtag Englishmen—first buccaneers, then log-cutters, finally plantation operators. None what you could call respectable.

It was a geographic division as well: swamps, jungle, and mountains cut off the coast from the Spanish highlands. The Spanish just never felt comfortable with the environment—only the Brits and a few of their American spin-offs could thrive in such seediness. So it was left to gringos such as Francis Drake, Henry Morgan, William Walker, and later on Sam (the Banana Man) Zemurray, the founder of United Fruit. Where the British went, there too came their slaves. So over the centuries the coast became mostly black and English-speaking, although these days the countries (except Belize) are slowly homogenizing themselves Ladino, as the indigenous Spanish culture is loosely called.

Gringo-sponsored revolutions have traditionally begun on this coast (against the nationalist Zelaya in Nicaragua in 1909; against a liberal anti–United Fruit regime in Honduras in 1910).

Oliver North targeted Puerto Cabezas, in Nicaragua, as the Contras' first beachhead. So it goes.

A CLEAR, COOL, easy northeast breeze carried us south from Punta Gorda, making us wonder, and not for the first time, just how long the total easiness we'd had so far was going to last. When you have no problems on a boat it's time to worry: The problems must be saving themselves up so they can all happen at once. We knew this from our reading, at least.

Columbus, for example, had made landfall on his disastrous last voyage 100 or so miles east of here on the coast of Honduras. It took him 28 days to beat 170 miles to the eastward. "Other tempests I have seen, but none that lasted so long or as grim as this." He was a broken man by the time he made it home and observed that he had had more trouble on that trip than on the other three put together.

But for us . . . blue skies and gentle trades, even though by now we were deep into the season of the northers: winter cold fronts sweeping down from the United States that can generate fifty knot winds for up to a week. We listened to the shortwave weather from the Portsmouth, Virginia, Coast Guard station every morning, wondering why those big blows seemed to be avoiding us.

The shoreline faded west into the swamps of the Sarstoon River between Guatemala and Belize and then began to rise again into the high ground at the mouth of the Río Dulce . . . the Gentle River . . . which in Stephens's and Catherwood's time was the only way into the interior of Central America: the old Spanish trade route to Antigua in the Guatemalan highlands.

We found the sea buoy and crossed the six-foot bar on the recommended heading of 225 degrees, lining up the *Lord Jim*'s heavy bowsprit with the chasm in the mountains where the river exited into a large bay. We cleared the bar without touching. The mountains rose and receded all around into reflected shades of gray and blue and on a low bluff on the north side we could see the fever port of Livingston. The only way you can get here is by sea.

BARRIODULCE said the sign on the grass-thatched hut on stilts over the water. Some girls sat on the veranda smoking and doing their nails. A teenage soldier with an AK-47 stood gravely on the gasoline dock. Through the window of the fanciest house visible (cement and tile, surrounded by a barbed wire-topped wall) we could see a boy and a girl doing some kind of wild dance. It was midafternoon.

The seedy old town—no-account in Stephens's time and after a brief banana-loading heyday in the late 1800s no-account again—was full of Germans. The little restaurants were packed with them ... they walked the streets in large groups, talking among themselves or to the local Garifuna bloods, but carefully (it seemed) never looking at us. They were young, long-haired, loose-clothed, Birkenstocked ... they looked like American Deadheads without the tie-dye.

We decided to follow one of them. Never looking back, he led us through a beachfront Garifuna settlement and finally disappeared into a compound surrounded by a white wall twenty feet high and topped with barbed wire. We knocked on the door. A dark-haired, white-skinned man opened it and looked at us.

"We just wanted to get a drink," we said in Spanish. "A Coke, a beer, whatever."

"Just for the guests," he said in English. He had a Spanish accent.

"Oh!" We made a great show of surprise. "Then this is a *hotel*!"

The man sighed.

"What's it called?" Susan asked. "The Four Walls?"

He nodded and stood there.

"See you later," I said. He was still standing there as we turned a corner in the path and walked into a little beachfront palapa next door. The owner was a Garifuna named Balthazar. He asked us if we were German. When we said we were American he served us drinks and told us that he and the rest of the people who lived along the beach had plans to burn down or blow up the hotel.

"Why would you want to do that?"

"Those people, mahn, they don't like us. They live in our place but they don't like us. Why they live here, then?"

"What's the name of it?"

"The fucking Flamingo."

A little while later, three younger Garifuna came in and sat at the other table. One was very drunk or stoned . . . his eyes kept rolling up in his head. He kept talking about burning down the Flamingo and every time he did his two friends would look at us and laugh apologetically.

"Rastaman is dead, mahn," they told him.

Susan and I began to speculate about his watch: whether or not it was a real gold Rolex. "Just a friendly argument," I told him. "She thinks it is. A Rolex."

"Argument?" He was suspicious.

"Well, not really an argument. More of a disagreement."

"Welllll . . ." He grinned at his friends. "It is, and it isn't. I had a very good friend, you see . . . We became such good friends that when he left . . . he gave me the watch."

"Is it a Rolex?"

"Yes."

"Ah!" I smiled. "Then I lose. She was right."

All three of them watched us without smiling back.

Beside the Germans, the streets were full of Garifuna children dressed in Mayan Indian *huipiles* (embroidered blouses) and *cortas* (skirts). They were escorted by their mothers, also in Mayan costume. Everyone was having a great time admiring each other. Groups of teenage bloods with ghetto blasters jostled past, their eyes and teeth glowing with mischief. It was *El Día de Guadalupe*, Santa Guadeloupe's Day ... "the day of the children" or "the day of the Indians" depending on who you asked.

There was dancing in the indoor athletic stadium. Punta. The temperature and the humidity were well over one hundred. And there were hundreds of shiny blue-black Garifuna of all ages whirling clockwise to the punta in their traditional Mayan costumes. Of course this was the coast and there were no real Mayans around; they were up in the mountains where they belonged.

The couple next to us had a Jack Russell terrier named Heinz. The dog came from Cuba. The man had gray hair and sad, distant blue eyes like weathered glacial ice. The much younger woman was stunningly olive, smooth and sleek as a racehorse, her hair in a perfect mousse, her body in a spangled wraparound. They owned the black steel ketch flying a German flag we had seen anchored off the pier.

We asked them about all the German hippies in town.

"We call them *Aussteiger*," the blue-eyed man said coolly. "Those who step out."

"What is it, a movement of some kind in Germany now?"

"No, they are bored. They have plenty of money and they are just bored."

The two had built the ketch themselves, sailed around the world on her twice, and were now heading back to Düsseldorf. They were bored with sailing ... she in particular looked like the kind of person who would bore easily: In fact we couldn't begin to imagine how she'd managed two circumnavigations.

"How long does it take to sail around the world?"

"Depends how long you stay in one place."

In Germany, the first few cracks were appearing in the Berlin Wall. East Germans, for the first time, were being allowed to travel at all.

T HE FOUR of us ended up at the Barriodulce. A Mexican
norteño waltz was on the jukebox and the place was full of
girls. One of them came over and asked the blue-eyed man if he
would mind if she touched the woman's hair. He shook his head.
She touched the hair gently and giggled.

The blue-eyed man waltzed beautifully with Susan, formal
German steps as if he were in the court of Kaiser Wilhelm II. I
told the woman my waltzing was terrible (no false modesty
there), and in no time at all she was with a big Ladino in a Bruce
Springsteen T-shirt with no sleeves. She tied Heinz's leash to the
blue-eyed man's chair.

The top half of the Ladino's body declined backwards at
something like a forty-five-degree angle. His loose T-shirt hung
straight down from his big shoulders. His right leg was somewhere out in front, fitting neatly in between hers; his left leg bore
the weight of the whole thing. His hips telegraphed all the moves,
so she was basically dancing with the hips, a pair of hands, and a
thigh. They watched each other without expression across three
or four feet of empty air.

We had a hard time looking at the blue-eyed man's face after
they'd danced a few more numbers without sitting down. We
didn't want to be caught staring. On the other hand we were very
curious to see. We tried to be as inconspicuous about it as possible
but he did catch us, smiled sadly and distantly, and nodded.

"WELL, NOW we know how she did it," Susan said as
we lay in the hammock on the *Lord Jim*'s foredeck,
watched the moon rise, and listened to the ongoing Mexican
music from the Barriodulce.

The veranda of the Barriodulce now was crowded with men and girls making their assignations. The young couple in the fancy house was continuing their wild dance. Or maybe it was another couple. Anyway, it wasn't dancing. We could see, looking from the dark into the brightly lit room, that it was a game of Ping-Pong.

JOHN LLOYD Stephens writes, in his usual graphically ardent fashion:

A narrow opening in a rampart of mountains wooed us on. On each side, rising perpendicularly from three to four hundred feet, was a wall of living green. Trees grew from the water's edge, with dense, unbroken foliage, to the top; not a spot of barrenness was to be seen; and on both sides, from the tops of the highest trees, long tendrils descended to the water, as if to drink and carry life to the trunks that bore them. It was, as its name imports, a Rio Dolce, a fairy scene of Titan land, combining exquisite beauty with colossal grandeur.

Well why not? Things were pretty much the same as the *Lord Jim* penetrated that same narrow opening 150 years later . . . and the fact that a fine rain was falling and mist shrouded the tops of the cliffs did not detract in the slightest. Another plus: Where Stephens only saw pelicans we saw white egrets with their choppy, paddle-shaped wings vivid against the green and six-foot oropendula (a big loud tropical oriole) nests suspended like scrotums from the high tree limbs. The vegetable green water was eighty feet deep in some of the bends, which you went around with the pleasant feeling that there was something even better waiting for you in the next stretch. Here and there was a grass shack on stilts or a fisherman in a *cayuco* ignoring the light drizzle, his hands flying in the old sign language of hand-lining.

We anchored in midafternoon in a deserted little cove within earshot of the ringing jungle. The rain was heavier, so we set the raincatcher and watched sweet water pouring into our tanks. It gave us a nice feeling of accomplishment even though we were just sitting there counting egrets.

Dreams on a boat are very strong. They can color your whole day, whereas on land you (at least I) tend to forget them in an hour or so. That night, with the soft, windless rain whispering on the deck a foot or so above my head, I had an art dream. Norman Mailer and I were arranging a flock of multicolored sheep over a huge green landscape . . . that is, each sheep had its own color but every color in the spectrum was represented. Indigo sheep: Imagine it! Mailer and I were working well together; each of us seemed to know instinctively what the other wanted and what was going to turn out best. We *arranged* those sheep all night in very significant patterns, calling directions to each other over the noise of their bleating and never making a false move.

When I woke up in the morning I felt as if I could write *The Naked and the Dead* in my sleep . . . which was nice, after the last two years of undifferentiated grayness and 250 pages of unpublishable manuscript. And when I went on deck the strange landscape arranged itself in patterns that were at least as significant as those carefully placed multicolored sheep.

Stephens and Catherwood might have felt the same hallucinatory exaltation if they had seen what we saw near the beginning of the Río Dulce twenty-five miles from the sea where it exits Lake Izabal. Up to then, everything had pretty much fit their description. Then, quite suddenly, we began to wonder if we weren't approaching Key Biscayne.

One can imagine the way Stephens might have written it:

Lining the tranquil shores were elaborate pleasure domes and castles, each clothed with a full bodice of verdant greensward.

In the skirts of these voluptuous structures was hiding a fantastic array of pleasure craft, ranging from tall sailing ships to power vessels run with a strange new form of fuel created deep within the earth from the decayed remains of dinosaurs . . .

The *Lord Jim* was left rolling in the wake of one of these same power vessels . . . under Panamanian registry, with a gaggle of teenage princesses passing suntan lotion back and forth on the foredeck, uniformed crew scurrying about with drinks for overweight ladies in deck chairs; and underneath the sunroof with his face in shadow a short, powerfully built man in Ray-Bans smoking a cigar and giving orders.

Maybe it was the president. Vinicio Cerezo, Guatemala's first civilian president in almost two decades, did keep a boat on the river and was said to enjoy life's little pleasures. But he was running scared this year, facing an election in which his own wife might run against him and a rejuvenated leftist guerrilla movement that some observers suspected of being financed by *narcotraficantes* intent on making Guatemala into the trendy new transshipment point. As if the election itself, if successfully carried out, wouldn't be the first time power was transferred from one elected president to another since 1950.

WE ANCHORED off a place called the Mañana Marina and rowed in. The evening video was *Top Gun* and everybody was speaking English with a Texas accent. There was going to be a potluck dinner on Sunday and someone was trying to organize a Christmas cruise to a harbor at the far end of Lake Izabal.

At the bar were Ward and Nancy, Chick and Barbara, two couples in their mid-fifties who had been cruising together for almost as long as they had been living on their boats: some five or six years. Not really cruising together but just running into each other over and over on the same leisurely route from the West Coast to the East Coast of the United States. They lobbed reminiscences back and forth like medicine balls, working out on them . . . the time the women got drunk in the Mariposa Hotel in Quepos, Costa Rica, leaving the men stranded on the boats for two days . . . the storm off Tehuantepec . . . the hassle in Las Hadas, Manzanillo, with the obnoxious movie producer . . . the reasons why one boat was expelled from Nicaragua and the other wasn't . . . until the men weaved off to their bunks. Then the women started on their own stories:

A man Barbara knew, his wife, their teenage daughter, and the man's best friend sailed together to the South Pacific. The man's best friend was the kind of guy who always knew best. He slowly drove the man crazy. The wife watched this growing craziness and finally jumped ship in Papeete. She returned to the States with the daughter, studied her ass off, and became a Master Mariner. Now she too knew everything. After a while she got a letter from the husband in Singapore: He was asking for a divorce so he could remarry. She could have the boat, he said, if she came to Singapore to get it. His new girlfriend hated boats; she was an airline stewardess on Pan Am. The ex-wife immediately got in touch with the man's best friend: They've been cruising on the boat ever since, sailing her back downwind from Singapore on the northern route.

"Nice story," Nancy said. "A real sea story. With a happy ending."

"Remind you of someone?" Barbara said.

"Who?"

"I asked you first, sweetie."

"No, I mean who in the *story.*"

"The man who always knows best, silly. Who did you think?"

Nancy just got up and opened two more beers. Salvavida was the Guatemalan brand name, meaning "lifesaver."

THE NEXT leg of Stephens and Catherwood's 150-mile route to Copán was overland and tricky. It took them almost two weeks ... traveling in early November 1839, the tail end of the rainy season. To begin with, they landed at the old trade-route port of Izabal on the shore of the lake and took a precipitous, muddy mule trail thirty miles over the Mico Mountains to the Motagua River valley:

> This was the great high road to the city of Guatimala. Almost all the travel and merchandise from Europe passes over it; and our guide said that the reason it was so bad was because it was traversed by so many mules ... with ten hours of the hardest riding I ever went through, we had made only twelve miles.

Now there was a bridge over the Río Dulce and a big new highway. The old trade route didn't show up on the new maps; neither did the port of Izabal. But still, the point was to follow them ... wasn't it?

A few old-timers at the Mañana Marina had heard of the old mule trail, although they knew of no one who had actually been over it. They didn't advise us trying it because this was an election year and kidnapping for ransom has traditionally been a popular fund-raising technique in Guatemala. And anyway, they said, there was "unrest" in the area.

Still, when Stephens and Catherwood made the trip, things were much rougher. Three different factions were fighting a running battle for power and a passport honored by one easily could have been an invitation to a necktie party by another. The fact that Stephens was traveling officially, as the latest United States chargé to the region, only seemed to heighten the risk: *"A fatality had hung over our diplomatic appointment to Central*

America: Mr. Williams, Mr. Shannon, Mr. Dewitt, Mr. Leggett, all who had ever held it, were dead."

Susan was inclined to take the modern route, which featured air-conditioned express buses. She reasoned that these were modern times, so it was appropriate.

I reasoned as follows: If Stephens and Catherwood could not only survive in those wild days but find time to carry on as shamelessly as Mrs. Catherwood claimed they did, surely we too ... etc., etc. It was our first "disagreement" this trip; I won only by appealing to her Bostonian sense of family. *We would be following in the footsteps of my ancestor.*

We packed sleeping hammocks because we had heard that sleeping on the floors of native huts was a good way to get Chagas' disease, the incurable beetle-transmitted wasting malady which eventually killed Charles Darwin. But it was a month later in the year for us than for Stephens and Catherwood (December instead of November), so we didn't have to worry about the rains. And after all, it was only a thirty-mile hike before we hit the highway on the other side of the mountains, so we packed supplies for two days ... the same time it had taken them.

Leaving the *Lord Jim* (at least) safe at the Mañana Marina, we hired a *cayuco* to take us twenty-five miles across the lake to Izabal. The *cayuquero* assured us there were still people living there, although skeptics at the marina warned he might just want the fare.

S O WE found it reassuring to be surrounded by a large, friendly crowd when we landed on the beach in front of the ruined stone customhouse and a scattering of thatched huts. We were apparently the first gringos to visit the place in years. An old man eagerly showed us artifacts from the good old days, including a stone whiskey flask inscribed "Stephens-London." Remembering that Stephens himself had bought the entire ruin of Copán for $50, we bargained desperately . . . but times had changed: He wouldn't go under $100. It was out of our range.

We fell in with a handsome, thirtyish woman named Nora who wanted to know all about life in the United States. We wanted to know about the trail. We were speaking in Spanish for a change since we were out of the English-speaking coastal belt.

Even though my Spanish isn't too bad, I still have the widespread gringo skepticism of this parallel world of baroque phraseology, endlessly subtle double entendres, insults and/or compliments that can mean instant death if said in the wrong tone at the wrong time. Above all, I'm skeptical of all "objective" observations about quantifiable phenomena. It all needs to be somehow certified . . . and I have reason to believe that Spanish-speaking folks feel the same way themselves.

"Is it still possible to pass over the trail?" I asked Nora.

"Yes . . . yes, no problem. Very easy."

"Is it very long?"

"No. Only a few hours."

"A few *hours?* I thought it was thirty miles."

"Well, maybe it will take longer."

"But it's passable?"

"Oh, yes."

"That's good. We want to go tomorrow."

She looked truly shocked. "You want to go? *You?*"

"Yes, *claro.* That's why we're here. We want to leave early tomorrow and cross over to the River Motagua."

"Good God. Wait a minute." She rushed off, apparently to find someone who might actually know something.

The ascent began precipitously, and by an extraordinary passage. It was a narrow gulley, worn by the tracks of the mules and the washing of mountain torrents so deep that the sides were over our heads and so narrow we could barely pass without touching . . . For five long hours we were dragged through mudholes, squeezed in gulleys, knocked against trees, and tumbled over roots; every step required care and great physical exertion; and, withal, I felt that our inglorious epitaph might be, "tossed over the head of a mule, brained by the trunk of a mahogany tree, and buried in the mud of the Mico Mountain.

Of course it was Catherwood who fell off his mule, not Stephens; but let that pass. The succession of people that Nora brought back to tell us about the trail all seemed to be telling us different things, but at least none of them mentioned "unrest." Neither of us knew the Spanish word for it, anyway.

In the end, I argued, the only thing to do was to do it and hope for the best. That's travel, after all. Isn't it?

"Your kind of travel, anyway," Susan said. And I was quick to thank her for being so indulgent.

Nora (who had a lively three-year-old daughter named Monica and no husband in sight) offered us hammock space in her little cement-block house, dinner, breakfast . . . and found someone to take us to the start of the trail at 5:30 the next morning. We sat up late with her and her best friend Dora (two daughters, no husband), watching the children play tag in the grassy lanes, and discussed the travel picture from their point of view.

FROM THE point of view of most people we talked to in Central America, the travel picture was both very simple and very complicated: the coyote route into the United States. Outside of every U.S. embassy in every Central American capital we visited, lines of the hopeful stretched twice around the block. To get the coveted visa they only had to prove they were not planning to stay for good, but under the jaundiced eye of U.S.

consulary experts less than half were convincing. For the rest: the coyote route.

The coyote route from Izabal cost about $800 U.S. The local coyote was a Mexican who lived in the next town over on the lakeshore. "He has hundreds of girls," Nora said, half in disgust, half in admiration. "Girls all over. Big house. He even has a boat for waterskiing."

Not too long ago, this coyote set out with a group of twenty local Guatemalans. They handed over their money, took buses up into the remote Petén district in the northeast, walked through the bush across the Mexican border into Chiapas, and were issued enough Mexican pesos for bus fare to Veracruz, on the Mexican gulf coast. They would divide up, take different buses, and reconvene at a certain address to continue the route.

No such address existed, or if it did exist not one of the twenty travelers could find it. They wandered around Veracruz, searching, until their pesos ran out. The locals there, it seemed, were not unused to their predicament. In fact, they found it amusing. The Guatemalans were the butt of many ribald Mexican jokes. "Only one person in all of Mexico was nice to them," Dora said. That person gave them food, shelter, and advice: Go back to your village, find this worthless coyote, and beat him until he returns your money.

"And did they?"

Dora shrugged. "Of course not. They were just *campesinos*. This man is rich, strong, and dangerous. And he has many friends."

"But people continue to go with him? Why?"

Now she laughed in real amusement. "*Claro,* because he is the only one. And sometimes they make it, you know. Yes. Sometimes they make it."

Sometimes *they* made it to America. But would *we* make it to Copán?

W E SET off before dawn in the company of the owner of the only store in Izabal, who went into the jungle every week to prospect for gold. He was saving the gold to pay the Mexican coyote. Some time ago, he said, he had had a good job in a car wash in Los Angeles. He had returned to take care of his mother, who died last year. Now he wanted to go back to the car wash . . . he was saving an ounce of gold every month.

It was still dark, but the town's grassy lanes were filled with *campesinos* carrying machetes in one hand and their lunch (rice and fish or meat) tied up in a banana leaf in the other. We followed them through mist-shrouded fields and across tree-trunk bridges as a Sistine Choir of jungle birds began to herald the dawn. The gold prospector showed us a little gate in the farthest field, nodded his head and jerked his thumb. "Well, be careful and maybe I'll see you sometime in New York."

"We hope so."

At eight o'clock Mr. C and I mounted, each armed with a brace of pistols and a large hunting knife, which we carried in a belt around the body. Augustin carried pistols and a sword; our principal muleteer, who was mounted, carried a machete and a pair of murderous spurs, with rowels two inches long, on his naked heels; and two other muleteers accompanied us on foot, each carrying a gun . . .

That was then. This was now . . . and the extent of our armament was a Swiss Army knife. But the trail was pretty much the same, with ten-foot-high sides and good old slippery deep mud that we slogged through on foot instead of on muleback like Stephens and Catherwood. Stephens said the mud was blue: It was actually brown. He said it was as deep as a mule's leg . . . for us, it was only about two feet deep. But since he was on a mule, he didn't come into the same kind of contact with it that we did: I can report also that the mud was clayey, so that the standing water was never absorbed, and that it made a perfect seal around your boots so that you couldn't pull them out of it very easily. From high on his mule's back, Stephens was free to look around him and see other things. Our world was the sky above and the mud below . . . and a lot of the time you could barely see the sky.

ONGOING PROBLEMS with the chief muleteer, in fact, turn out to be a kind of *leitmotif* in Stephens's book:

All day he (the chief muleteer) had been particularly furious with the mules, and they had been particularly perverse, and now they had gone astray; and it was an hour before we heard his spiteful voice, loading them with curses.

And:

I ordered the muleteer to saddle the mules; but the rascal enjoyed our confusion, and positively refused to saddle his beasts that day.

And:

As I moved through, a flash rose from under my feet, and a petard exploded so near that the powder singed me; and, turning around, I saw hurrying away my rascally muleteer.

The muleteer's recurrent "surliness" and "brutality" goes beyond a mere personality quirk, and the careful reader has to ask himself what is really going on. In line with Mrs. Catherwood's revelations, one theory fits perfectly. There is a woman involved. One who is somehow close to the muleteer but who is also attractive to Stephens or Catherwood: his daughter. Surely the situation could have been as follows: Stephens and/or Catherwood hired the daughter in some nominal capacity on the trip (say, assistant cook) and the cash was so good the muleteer couldn't say no. This theory is only reinforced by the fact that the daughter is never mentioned in Stephens's book.

M EANWHILE, THINGS with *my* woman were on the dicey side. We were wearing jeans and long-sleeved shirts against the brush and insects. Half an hour up the trail the shirts were as wet as if we'd been swimming in them and the jeans were brown to mid-thigh with mud. Even though we were now high on the mountain, we could still only see the sides of the trail and the branches right above them. The lighting was dark green with occasional spears of bright sun.

Were we the first gringos on the trail since 1839? Hardly likely . . . but still, one had an eerie feeling that around some corner we'd come across my relative floundering in the muck and telling anyone within earshot that (as Stephens allows him the rare quote) if he'd known ahead of time how bad the trail would be, Stephens would be traveling alone. Now here is continuity for you: 150 years later Susan was saying exactly the same things.

I had gotten ahead, and sat down at a fork in the trail to wait. In no time at all I heard the suck-suck-suck of quick footsteps in deep mud; it wasn't Susan. Susan's pace is slow but sure, as long as she knows how far she has to go. If the trip is open-ended, the way I tend to like it, she dawdles and balks.

It was an old man and a boy, roaring along through the mud as if the trail were a city sidewalk.

"Where are you going?"

"Río Motagua. Did you see a woman back there?"

They smiled and nodded.

"How far?"

"Not too far."

"How did she look?"

"Dirty," the old man said. He was tall and thin, with pale skin and a hooked, pure-blooded Spanish nose.

"And angry," the boy said.

The boy and the old man looked at each other. "This is your wife?" the old man asked.

I said yes, even though Susan and I aren't married. Times have changed since Stephens's day but, as I said, this trail and immediate environs seemed mired in the past.

Without my asking, they sat down with me to wait. We had the usual inconclusive but entertaining discussion of time and distance. After a while we began to hear Susan's slow steps and see the glimmering of her purple mosquito-proof shirt through the curtain of green. "Here she comes," the boy said, his eyes wide.

"Just ask them how far it is to the top," Susan said when she drew abreast, wet, muddy, and crimson of face . . . indeed a frightening figure.

"*I did.*"

"*. . .*"

I felt her eyes on me. "They say the path to the left is a short-cut. But it could be washed out. Why don't I follow them a little way up, and see if it looks okay. I'll shout back. If it's not okay, just follow the main trail. We'll meet up back where they join."

She slapped a mosquito on her forehead. "Let me get this straight. You're suggesting you go off with these . . . people . . . in one direction while I go off by myself in another? In *this?*"

"In what?"

"This godforsaken . . . who are these people?"

"Just . . . peasants. I guess. They seem okay."

"Peasants my ass."

"Well . . . we don't have to do it. But it might save a lot of time." This point carried.

THE SHORTCUT turned out to be a creek bed. Rushing water had scoured out huge gullies and high banks. We clambered up and down them for a while, and I decided that to invite Susan up here would be cruel and unusual for both of us . . . and climbing down again would be cruel to me. I shouted back and heard her faint scream of insult or acquiescence on taking the main trail. But really I had no reason to doubt what I'd been told: The main trail climbed up in big, gentle loops; this was just a shortcut across one of them.

Then I turned my attention to keeping up with the incredibly fit old man and the mountain goat–like boy and a few hours or years later came out at the bottom of an almost perpendicular clearing. Men with machetes were making it larger: It was a *milpa,* a field that would be used for growing corn or other crops until the soil gave out (after maybe one or two seasons) and then abandoned.

The crop here consisted of seven- or eight-foot-tall bushy plants with resinous seed clusters and groups of five long, fern-like leaves. I tried to pretend that I hadn't seen it . . . and even if I had seen it, didn't know what it was. The men with machetes seemed to be pretending the same about me.

"A lot of work." The old man smiled. "They are just *campesinos.*"

I tried to assume an expression that indicated no particular approval, censure, or much interest of any kind. Out in the clearing, the direct sun fell on us like boiling rain.

"You know prices are very good now. Fifteen hundred quetzals (about $600) per pound."

"I don't know anything about it."

"And the prices in the United States? How are they?"

"I don't know." I shrugged and grinned. "We are just tourists. Just walking."

"And José? How is he?"

"I don't know. We don't know José."

"José from New York? You don't know him?"

"I'm very sorry, but I don't know him. We are just walking."

The old man watched me calmly. The boy drifted off to talk to one of the machete men.

"Where is the main trail?" I asked after a while.

"Your wife . . . she is just walking, too?"

"*Claro que sí.*"

"To the Río Motagua?"

"Yes."

"And why do you come this way? You know there is a highway."

"This is the old Spanish road. We are following in the footsteps of my great-great-grandfather. He came over this same road in 1839."

The old man's face seemed gradually to lose some kind of hardened covering that I hadn't noticed until I saw it go. "Spanish blood, then."

"*Claro que sí.*"

"And may one inquire your great-great-grandfather's name?"

"Aguirre. Federico Jesús Aguirre Catherwood. His mother was English." It was at least half true.

"Aguirre . . . come, I think we'd better go from here. Let's find your wife."

A MILE BACK down the main trail we found Susan in the company of two young Ladinos wearing revolvers Western-style in beat-up leather holsters. Susan was sitting on a fallen tree and the young men were standing in front of her like two schoolkids in front of their homeroom teacher. "I kept telling them to go find you, but they just keep hanging around. I think I sprained my knee."

The old man and the Ladinos talked in rapid Spanish. "I can barely walk," Susan said. "How are we going to get out of here?"

"I don't know."

"Well, can't they help us?"

"It's . . . a little touchy."

"*What do you mean, a little touchy.*" She has always had a short fuse. It was burning down fast. I looked at the men, looked back at her, and shook my head.

"I . . ."

"Your wife is hurt," the old man was saying.

"Yes. Her knee. She can't walk."

"No problem. There is a road near here. We have a car. We'll give you a ride." His smile seemed ominously friendly.

"A ride?" I asked shakily. "Where to?"

"What do you mean, where to?" Susan said. "*Just out of here.*"

"Look . . . you don't . . ."

"You are going to the Río Motagua. We'll take you to the Río Motagua," the old man said. "*They'll* take you. I need to stay here. But," he tapped his chest with his forefinger, "we are brothers, you and I. You have seen nothing. Am I right?"

"What is he talking about?" Susan said.

"Absolutely right. On all my honor."

"And what is your name, señor?"

"Gordon. Gordon Aguirre."

"*Gordon Aguirre?*" It was the last straw for Susan, but the old man's mind was already back in the milpa.

"Señor Aguirre. And señora. It has been a pleasure. And

now permit me." He turned and roared off in that incredible ground-covering gait.

THE CAR turned out to be an olive-drab military Jeep with a two-way radio. The two young men sat in front. We drove over the top of the mountain and down the other side on a freshly bulldozed road that must have cost someone a fortune to build.

I looked at Susan and smiled. "What luck, huh?"

"Will you please tell me what's going on?"

Mr. C. and I were in a rather awkward predicament for the night. The general reception room contained three beds, made of strips of cowhide interlaced. The don occupied one; he had not much undressing to do, but what little he had, he did by pulling off his shirt. Another bed was at the foot of my hammock. I was dozing, when I opened my eyes, and saw a girl about seventeen sitting sideway upon it, smoking a cigar. She had a piece of striped cotton cloth tied around her waist and falling below her knees; the rest of her dress was the same which Nature bestows alike upon the belle of fashionable life and the poorest girl; in other words, it was the same as that of the don's wife, with the exception of the beads. At first I thought it was something I had conjured up in a dream; and as I waked up perhaps I raised my head, for she gave a few quick puffs of her cigar, drew a cotton sheet over her head and shoulders, and lay down to sleep. I endeavoured to do the same. I called to mind the proverb, that "travelling makes strange bedfellows." I had slept pellmell with Greeks, Turks, and Arabs. I was beginning a journey in a new country; it was my duty to conform to the customs of the people; to be prepared for the worst, and submit with resignation to whatever might befall me . . .

This is about as explicit as Stephens gets . . . after all, it was the nineteenth-century. Still, that "submit with resignation" is a nice turn, you have to admit.

S TRANGE BEDFELLOWS, indeed. We were in a little inn just off the highway through the Río Motagua valley where the two young men with revolvers had dropped us, probably no more than a beer bottle's throw from where Stephens and Catherwood indulged themselves. We'd washed down a quick dinner of rice and beans with about four beers apiece and fallen into bed . . . pretty happy that the hike was over and done with even though I noticed that the farther Susan got from the mud the better her knee seemed to be.

We had a plywood cubicle that seemed to function as an echo chamber, magnifying the noises from the rest of the hotel and even creating some new ones. Outside in the courtyard a flock of vicious geese guarded the entrance to the only bathroom. A TV was playing somewhere: "The Flintstones," in Spanish.

In the next cubicle a man and a woman were arguing in New York accents. They too were heading to the Copán ruins which were a few miles over the border in Honduras: You could get tourist passes from both countries enabling you to spend a few days at the ruins and return to Guatemala without having to go through formal entry procedures.

The man was supposed to have found out the bus schedule, but something had gone wrong.

"That's the trouble with you, Dan," the woman said. Her voice was hoarse from overuse. "It's always been the trouble. And it always will be. Because you never learn. Do you?"

"No, Lenore. I never learn." The man's voice was hoarse too, but tired.

"I think you should go to a psychiatrist," the woman said. "I think it's pathological."

"Right, Lenore . . ."

"Your mother did it to you. And you still go crawling back to her. *Mama's little boy.*"

". . ."

"Well, I'll tell you one thing, Dan. I'm going to be out at that bus stop at five in the morning. And I'm going to get on the first one that comes along. Because I want to *get* there sometime in this century, *little boy.*"

I dropped one of my hiking boots on the floor. It sounded as if it weighed 100 pounds. We could feel the two of them listening and tried to think of something witty to say but we were just too tired.

OUT IN the courtyard the next morning I saw the woman trying to get past the geese into the bathroom. She was tall, thin, dark-haired, and her face would have been attractive with a good smile instead of the big-city grimace she had. She was wearing a tank top with no bra and her breasts no doubt had strained many eyeballs in Central America. The geese had their necks stretched toward her and sounded like rusty gate hinges being pried open.

"What do they want from me?" she said. "My God, it's worse than Bloomingdale's."

"Just push right through like you would at Bloomingdale's."

"Forget about it. They'll tear me to pieces."

"They don't have teeth."

"How do you know? You checked inside their mouths?"

I pushed through the geese myself, went inside the bathroom, and closed the door. They hardly noticed me: They were imprinted on the woman. In a few minutes I could hear her telling her boyfriend that I'd just pushed in ahead of her.

When I came out, the two of them were still standing there in front of the geese. The boyfriend was tall, thin, and bald with pale skin and a black heavy beard. They didn't look at me. "Okay, big shot," the woman said. "Now gettem *outta* here."

"Look, Lenore . . ."

"*I need to get in that bathroom.*"

"Excuse me," I said. "Does anybody know what time the bus leaves for Copán?"

I T TURNED out there were many buses . . . they left every few minutes, each one hand packed by beefy conductors who sweated and strained as they forced absolutely the last possible passenger into place. Stephens and Catherwood would have loved it: I'm sure they both were well acquainted with the nineteenth-century French concept of *frottage:* sexual contact obtained by the "accidental" rubbing of the active party against the oblivious one.

Oh, and by the way: Their outraged muleteer finally got a kind of revenge. He halted the muletrain in a tiny village called Comotan, just short of the Honduran border, and apparently reported his employers to the local authorities as spies or undesirable foreign agents. In the middle of the night they were arrested by "a band of cowardly ruffians" and locked up in the government office building. *"My belief is, that if we had quailed at all, and had not kept up a high, threatening tone to the last, we should not have been set free."* But set free they were, and the next day crossed over into Honduras, Copán, and immortality.

W HAT WITH everything else that was going on, one tends to forget that Stephens's primary reason for being in the area was to establish a relationship for the United States with whatever governments he could find. It was an interesting period: For sixteen years, since they declared independence from Spain in 1823, the "United Provinces of Central America" had been shakily united. Now the union was breaking up, and the adolescent United States was beginning to flex its muscles. Manifest Destiny was right around the corner, and Stephens was its point man. He traveled some 3,000 miles (while Catherwood was back in the ruins) in search of a leader to present his credentials to, but couldn't find him. The best candidate, Gen. Francisco Morazán of Honduras, who was trying to reunite the provinces, was defeated:

> He is now fallen and in exile, probably forever, under sentence of death if he returns; all the truckling worshippers of a rising sun are blasting his name and memory; but I verily believe, and I know I shall bring down upon me the indignation of the whole Central party by the assertion, I verily believe they have driven from their shores the best man in Central America.

History marches on. By the time we arrived at the Honduran border on a late afternoon in mid-December 1990, (by taxi: We'd missed the last of five bus changes in nine hours and maybe sixty miles) the lines were firmly drawn: two flags, two guard posts, a strip of no-man's-land in between, and on the Honduran side soldiers in what looked like hand-me-down U.S. Army fatigues carrying M-16s. The German *Aussteiger* we'd shared the taxi with was turned away because his passport showed entry to several communist countries. Good old Honduras: home of the Contras, some 1,200 U.S. troops (according to the U.S. Embassy), and the old United Fruit Company (now Chiquita Banana).

Once again, though, big changes were right around the corner. This was December. In two months the Sandinistas would be out of office in Nicaragua, the Iron Curtain would have crumbled, and the only communist country worth mentioning would be Cuba. U.S. aid to Honduras would be slashed and the Contras would be surrendering their arms. So it goes, as they used to say.

As for the banana: It is still the world's most popular fruit, and Honduras and Panama are still the world's most important banana-growing countries. But these days banana giants like the old United Fruit company have fragmented, pulled in their horns, and lowered their visibility. Other crops (such as African palm oil) have grown in importance. The last real banana revolution was in Guatemala in 1954, when United Fruit perceived Pres. Jacobo Arbenz Guzmán as hostile to its interests and engineered his downfall through the CIA.

C OPÁN WAS a pleasant place to catch up on the news. The tourist industry which originally built it was keeping it in quaint good shape; there were luscious golden hills surrounding it, clear rivers, and the pleasantly dry, coolish climate (altitude was over 3,000 feet) reminded us of Santa Barbara. We were eating a breakfast of spicy *huevos rancheros* at the *Castillo de Dracula lonchería* and trying to overhear the radio announcer on the little portable propped on our neighbor's table. Something about United States troops in Panama.

"What's happening?" we asked when the music came back on.

He looked at us carefully. *Americanos.*

"Un problema."

Back at our hotel after breakfast, we noticed the New York couple arguing with the desk clerk over exchange rates. We hadn't heard them during the night: Either they were just arriving now or the soundproofing was better.

"Did you have a good trip?"

The man shrugged.

"What's happening in Panama, anyway?"

They both looked at us suspiciously.

"Maybe it was an invasion," I said. "You haven't heard about it?"

"So who invaded what?" the woman said after a little while.

"I think we invaded them."

"What *we?* What are you talking?"

"We. The United States. Bush. Troops."

"So that punk Noriega got what he deserved. So what else is new."

They wanted to split the cab fare out to the ruins but we decided to walk. *So what else is new?* Locusts sang in the golden grass and birds twittered from the huge ceiba trees and we tried our best to imagine the United States' invasion of Panama and how it might relate to Stephens's and Catherwood's discovery of the ruins 150 years earlier.

It lay before us like a shattered bark in the midst of the ocean, her masts gone, her name effaced, her crew perished, and none to tell whence she came, to whom she belonged, how long on her voyage, or what had caused her destruction; her lost people to be traced only by some fancied resemblance in the construction of the vessel, and, perhaps, never to be known at all. The place where we sat, was it a citadel from which an unknown people had sounded the trumpet of war? or a temple for the worship of the God of peace? or did the inhabitants worship the idols made with their own hands, and offer sacrifices on the stones before them? All was mystery, dark, impenetrable mystery, and every circumstance increased it.

Somehow the New York couple, who had gotten there ahead of us in the cab, only increased the impact of the ruins. Once they were in the ruins, they were changed ... it was as amazing to see as if the Empire State Building had suddenly turned bright green.

We saw them on the other side of the Great Plaza, a flat grassy area larger than two football fields and set at wide intervals with fourteen-foot-high slabs of stone carved back and front into the shape of huge ornamented figures of men and women. They were sitting on a low wall, a guidebook resting on their knees and the man's arm around the woman's shoulders. In front of them was a 100-foot-high pyramid with steps as large as sofas, supporting in its turn a 100-foot-high ceiba tree. To their left was another pyramid, almost as high; every step of the stairway up the front was a different hieroglyph. Their mouths were open like two children.

THE NEW York couple hadn't wanted to pay for a guide ("We never use them.") so we had one to ourselves: Rafael Antonio, nineteen, born in Copán. Rafa, bright and ambitious, had wanted to become an archaeologist even though his father was a farmer because that's where the money was in Copán. All the gringo archaeologists were loaded, and there were always huge costly excavation projects under way.

But there was no academic program for the study of archaeology in Honduras. So Rafa got his degree in agronomy and had just been accepted for a two-year scholarship to the United States to study cattle-raising.

Meanwhile he works as a guide. He was interested to hear
that I was related to Frederick Catherwood: The name was famous, but he'd never read the book. We showed him a copy of
Incidents of Travel, with those incredible illustrations.

"But I *know* these objects." Now he was absolutely
amazed. "I know exactly where they are. Come on. I'll take you to
them."

We followed him with (I'll have to admit) just a touch of
proprietary feeling.

Our guide cleared a way with his machete, and we passed, as it
lay half buried in the earth, a large fragment of stone elab-
orately sculptured, and came to the angle of a structure with
steps on the sides, in form and appearance, so far as the trees
would enable us to make it out, like the sides of a pyramid.
Diverging from the base, and working our way through the
thick woods, we came upon a square stone column, about
fourteen feet high and three feet on each side, sculptured in
very bold relief, and on all four of the sides, from the base to
the top. The front was the figure of a man, curiously and richly
dressed, and the face, evidently a portrait, solemn, stern, and
well fitted to excite terror. The back was of a different design,
unlike anything we had ever seen before, and the sides were
covered with hieroglyphics. This our guide called an "Idol;"
and before it, at a distance of three feet, was a large block of
stone, also sculptured with figures and emblematical devices,
which he called an altar. The sight of this unexpected monument put at rest and once and forever, in our minds, all uncer-
tainty in regard to the character of American antiquities . . .

Many of the huge trees in and around the ruins had been left
standing, giving you the feeling that even after four generations
of clearing and excavation the whole thing could sink back into
the jungle overnight. The jungle was waiting, only a few feet
away, a taller, drier jungle than what we were used to on the
coast, but dense enough that the cleared paths through it looked
like tunnels.

Light slanted down through the trees in brilliant spears, illuminating large flying insects and tiny red and blue birds. Ahead of us, now clambering up the sofa-size steps of the giant pyramid, the New York couple looked weirdly reduced in size . . . as if they'd eaten too much of the shrinking side of the mushroom in *Alice in Wonderland.* The woman went first, with the man helping from below. Then she would turn around and pull him up after her.

After several hours absence, I returned to Mr. Catherwood, and reported upwards of fifty objects to be copied. I found him not so well pleased as I expected. He was standing with his feet in the mud, and was drawing with his gloves on to protect his hands from the *moschetoes.* As we feared, the designs were so intricate and complicated, the subjects so entirely new and unintelligible, that he (Catherwood) had great difficulty in drawing . . . The 'idol' seemed to defy his art . . .

By 1990, the mosquitoes had somehow been brought under control and didn't bother us much. Ditto the mud. The ruins, in fact, were luxuriously comfortable compared to what we were used to in the steamy lowlands. But in 1839 my relative stood there for two days, ill with *"a prospective attack of fever and ague or rheumatism,"* until he finally got the right slant of light. And when Rafa eagerly showed us the original subject of his first drawing—a stela (as the fourteen-foot-high 'idols' are called) of Yax Pac, Copán's last ruler—the original was . . . *disappointing.* It was exactly the same, down to the last fillip, scroll, effigy, ornamental creature, hieroglyph, eyeball, twist of lip, bend of finger, but just not as dramatic. Of course, it was 150 years later and the stone is soft.

M OST OF the mysteries that entranced Catherwood and Stephens unfortunately are now solved . . . we know the names of the gods and the kings, how they lived, what they thought, who they sacrificed, what sports they played, the design of their sanitary facilities, etc. Only one big question is left: why the city was abandoned in the first place. The population reached its peak around 820 and was completely gone by 1200. "Crime!" It was the woman from New York, behind us. We were standing in the Place of Jaguars, a large rectangular amphitheater surrounded by tiers of seats and dancing jaguars carved in stone and fronted by a pyramid from which the priests dispensed the word to the waiting multitudes. We were looking into the Sun King's eyes and noticing he had slit pupils like a jaguar's. "Things just got out of hand," she said. "And then there was chaos. The social order broke down. Everybody was out for themselves . . . and they turned back into savages."

"Lenore was mugged a week before we left," the man explained. "On Park Avenue. During rush hour."

"Dan . . ."

"Well you were, Lenore. You gotta start trying to deal with it."

"Okay." She handed me a few lempira notes. "We'll hire your guide for a minute. What does *he* say caused it?"

"Ritual mutilation of the sexual organs was what extincted these poor people," Rafa said jauntily, showing us what he said was a carving of a penis with blood dripping from it.

"There, you see?" she said to Dan. She turned and began to walk away. "Aren't you glad we saved our money?"

The ruins closed at five P.M. The New York couple and everybody else left. Susan was tired and went back to the hotel for a nap. But I, being a relative of the famous Catherwood, had gotten special permission to stay until dark.

I found the exact spot where Stephens and Catherwood sat on their first day *"and strove in vain to penetrate the mystery by which we were surrounded."* The mystery felt as close as night in the tropics, which falls so suddenly you hardly have time to breathe. Four generations of gringo scientists might have penetrated the mystery at this juncture in history, but that's daytime knowledge. And of course my relative remained as inscrutable as ever.

Now the mystery was silent; there were no evening birds singing in the huge trees. The light slanted across the Great Plaza a hundred feet below the top of the pyramid where I sat and the stelae cast Daliesque shadows on the grass. I blinked my eyes slowly and there were four silent deer grazing among the stelae.

"The steps were ornamented with sculpture, and on the south side, about halfway up, forced out of its place by roots, was a colossal head, evidently a portrait." I was staring into the huge face. The eyes were blank, but with laugh lines in the corners. The jaw was square. There were smile lines on the cheeks. The nose was broken (literally). The mouth was wry, straight, thin-lipped, a little open, showing two square teeth in the corners and a strange half-moustache. It was not talking.

The sun set behind the ring of hills. I walked into the sanctum sanctorum in the Place of Jaguars and prepared myself. When I felt ready I went out through the death's heads and huge snakes on the sculptured portals to where Frederick Catherwood waited to tell me some of the family secrets.

A THLETIC TEENAGE girls were doing handsprings on the brightly lighted village square in front of a busload of international hippies when I got back, thirsty for cold beer and news from Panama. I watched for a while anyway, then headed for the Tunkul Bar, down some steep steps at the bottom of a ravine, where there was supposed to be a television.

Things were lively: The slick-looking guide we had seen shepherding a fortyish American woman and her beautiful blonde daughter around the ruins was now tending bar; the beautiful blonde daughter was sitting on one of the bar stools and the mother was nowhere in sight. The rest of the stools were occupied and people were packed four deep behind them. Everybody was waiting for the news.

On my right was a well-dressed, light-skinned young Honduran who said he was a doctor in Tegucigalpa, the capital of Honduras. On *his* right were two beefy, hard-eyed Americans with heavy Boston accents who said they were in the Peace Corps. Yeah, sure.

"Do you get much time off from training?" the doctor asked the Peace Corps volunteers.

He asked me what I was doing; I asked him what *he* was doing. He said he was driving his BMW to Guatemala City for service because there were no good mechanics in Honduras. The visible parts of his body were covered with scars he said he had gotten motorcycle racing.

The news came on: 22,000 U.S. troops had taken Panama City from 15,000 Panamanian troops. U.S. casualties were fifteen dead, fifty-nine wounded. Panamanian casualties were not mentioned. Noriega was still at large, although a price of $1 million U.S. had been placed on his head. He had issued a statement calling on all nations to help him in the face of "brutal aggression."

"There's a drink here you should try," the doctor said to us suddenly. It was not sold over the bar so he sent a boy out for a flask of it. He said it was called *guaro*.

The flask had no label. The liquid inside was colorless. "I don't drink much anymore," the doctor said, pouring out double shots for all of us.

The liquor was raw and almost tasteless. The PCVs and I stopped after the second double, but the doctor had four straight. "Come on, gringitos," he said to us. "You must keep up."

After a while we saw that the TV screen was showing footage of helicopters in the jungle, napalm, fighter planes, GIs running and firing M-16s. It looked like a full-scale war. The doctor suddenly seemed very drunk. "My God," he muttered. "What are you doing to us now?"

There was something strange about the footage. I tried to pick it out through the haze of *guaro*. Finally I saw that the little brown-skinned figures had slanted eyes, and that most of the fields had water in them. The announcer spoke up, in English. Everybody in the Tunkul Bar was fascinated by the display of United States firepower but only the few who spoke English understood that what we were watching was indeed an HBO special on Vietnam.

THE NEW York couple was listlessly pawing through tourist trinkets in the little store across the street from the hotel when we came out the next morning. We could hear the words "junk," "overrated," "bus schedule" in the woman's voice. She was wearing a tight yellow jersey with NEW YORK REVIEW OF BOOKS printed in black letters across her breasts and a few young men of the town were standing around unobtrusively getting an eyeful.

"It was good for a day," she said to us as we went by. "Anymore than that, you're just wasting your time."

We shrugged and grinned.

"You guys going back?"

We nodded.

"What for?" She began to look worried.

"Oh, just more of the same."

She was reassured and turned back to the trinkets.

"What did you think of the stone hammock?" I asked. "Pretty amazing . . ."

"Stone hammock? Wha . . . ?"

"I couldn't believe it," I said. "All that weight, and you could move it with just a finger."

"...?..."

"Don't tell me you missed it. It was practically the first thing the guide showed us. The only thing was, we spent so much time there we have to go back today to see the rest."

Still it may have existed, and may be there still, broken and buried. The padre of Gualan told us he had seen it, and in our inquiries among the Indians we met with one who told us that he had heard his father say that *his* father, two generations back, had spoken of such a monument . . .

We had made a startling discovery the day before, pacing off Catherwood's original survey. It checked out exactly with the way things were except for one crucial inconsistency: The compass directions were reversed. North was actually south; east was actually west. This could have happened during printing but we knew Catherwood had closely overseen the whole process so it seemed unlikely.

He must have wanted it that way.

The Mayans lined the temple up due north. But in Catherwood's survey, it lined up due south. Thus we reasoned that due south was likely to be the direction to the stone hammock . . . "somewhere up in the hills," as Mrs. Catherwood had said in her letter.

We were pretty excited. I imagined how "The Catherwood Hammock" would look on TV and in the newspapers and wished my mother and my uncle could have been around.

Especially my mother. *I was the one who had been supposed to make her proud, to rescue her. And who was always disappointing.*

U SING THE huge ceiba tree growing out of the central pyramid of the ruins as a landmark to track due south from with our pocket hiking compass, we waded across the Copán

River and walked the farm roads into the hills as far as we could. When the farm roads petered out, we followed cattle trails. It was dry and not too hot: We felt energetic and optimistic. The long green grass in the fields rippled in a fresh breeze off the higher mountains. The dry oak leaves on the ground under the trees crackled underfoot and the sound of the locusts was the sound of summer at home where I grew up.

I THOUGHT OF the big sad house, the dusty attic on the warm fall day after my mother's death, the rosewood box in my grandfather's trunk, the page from my mother's diary: *"I guess they think I am not worthwhile, and they are right."* What had the torn-out fragment been doing there? What had it meant to my grandfather? Why had he done nothing about it? And what had my mother thought when she eventually found it there?

In the end, the Catherwood legacy was silence . . . and the tangible incompleteness of lives lived under that burden. Beside this, the image of the inscrutable Frederick philandering his way across Central America with his Rabelaisian buddy had always seemed a major step in the right direction.

Somehow, I imagined, rediscovering the hammock would resolve this legacy even further. Maybe after our fifteen minutes in the limelight, long-lost relatives would come forward to explain some of the gaps. Or maybe I'd simply care less. Maybe then, after the hammock was discovered, I'd be able for the first time to write a decent personal essay. Because maybe then I'd have a better idea of who I really was and where I came from.

My uncle Cummins Catherwood had served in World War II; *doing what?* His buddies in the fifties included people like Allen Dulles, the CIA director in the Eisenhower Administration. He had had a black cocker spaniel named Dean Acheson, after

Truman's Secretary of State. The Catherwood Foundation, which he had created, had been a conduit for CIA money to magazines, newspapers and student organizations abroad. Hadn't it? My uncle had been a great one for quips and pleasantries, but true to form as a real Catherwood, he had never really told me a thing.

Of course we had never discussed my mother. After she'd been killed in a car accident, we'd embraced and cried together for the first and last time and ever since then had been slightly embarrassed with each other. And I'd been scared, too, because looking into his eyes was exactly the same as looking into hers.

That was not something I did very often: Catherwood eyes tend to be small and indirect, mine included. And I had reason to believe that toward the end of her life my mother had been losing her mind. Some kind of terrible depression had been creeping over her, apparently the bitter dessert of the one thing I had been told about her all my life: *"You must remember she had a tragic childhood."*

THE NEW York couple were about the last people we wanted to see when we came down at dusk after eight hours of tramping the hills, but there they were in the hotel lobby, lolling on the uncomfortable chairs as if they were too tired to climb upstairs. For once the woman wasn't talking. I thought I saw real curiosity in her face for the first time as she watched us walk in and it occurred to me that the reason they were there was because they didn't want to miss us.

We nodded and kept up a fast pace as we moved by.

"Excuse me." She really didn't look angry. "Do you mind if I ask you a question?"

"Not at all."

"All right. What did you do it for?"

"What? I'm not sure I . . ."

"I'm not mad. I'd just like to know."

"Ahm . . . ah . . ."

"You're going to be surprised to hear this, but actually we owe you something for what you did. We'd like to thank you."

I tried hard to find anything in her voice but sincerity, and couldn't. "Well, you're welcome."

"We had quite a remarkable day, *thanks to you*. Didn't we, Dan? I don't think we'll ever forget it."

"That's . . . nice."

"I mean, we didn't find the hammock, of course . . ."

I nodded automatically.

"But Dan and I have decided to get married. We thought you should be the first people we told."

Dan was nodding and smiling.

"Well," Susan said. "That's wonderful."

"Yes," I said.

"You're wondering how it happened," the woman said. "I'm afraid we won't be able to tell you."

"It will have to remain a mystery," Dan said. "Kind of like the hammock itself."

W E WERE lying in bed, listening to a radio play Mexican *norteño* music up one of the side streets off the square. We were both good and tired, and somehow it felt very satisfying.

"You made that whole business up, didn't you?" Susan said.

"What are you talking about? You've read Stephen's book . . . it's all in there, about the hammock. You saw the directions were backward, everything."

"Just tell me this. Are you really related to Frederick Catherwood?"

"Yes. On my uncle's grave."

She didn't push any farther. We hadn't found the hammock either, not too surprisingly. What we had found, on the rim of the hills overlooking the village and the ruins, were places where huge blocks of stone had been quarried out for the construction. Some of them were still up there, for some reason abandoned.

On the face of the largest, carved in different hands, were two names: JOHN L. STEPHENS and FREDERICK CATHERWOOD.

> We remained all day on the top of the range. The close forest in which we had been labouring made us feel more sensibly the beauty of the extended view. On the top of the range was a quarried block. With the chay stone found among the ruins, and supposed to be the instrument of sculpture, we wrote our names upon it. They stand alone, and few will ever see them . . .

The rest was silence. I don't know why I expected anything different. But compared to Stephens's rough scrawl, my relative's grafitti was neatly and regularly carved and seemed in its own way to speak to me as personally as that diary fragment of my mother's: *Rescuing her had been impossible.*

When we first arrived we'd asked the director of the ruins about the carved signatures: He'd said that to his knowledge they'd never been found. We'd stumbled on them by accident, and before we left we put our hands on them and swore not to tell where they were. We took no pictures.

But the letters under my fingers were amazingly sharp and distinct and I felt I had found at least something of what I had been looking for. It was a family matter, after all, and maybe that's the best you can hope for in those things.

I was free to move on. Which was lucky, because Susan was getting tired of bowing to my ancestor and we had a lot of sailing left to do.

Three

Honduras

UDDENLY IT was mid-February and we were only in the ancient port city of Trujillo, halfway along the north coast of Honduras, where Columbus first made contact with the North American continent and later O. Henry had hid out for a couple of years fleeing embezzlement charges in the U.S. We'd hoped to be in Nicaragua for the elections February 25, but there wasn't a chance of making it; we'd had a hard time even getting where we were.

More than three months had passed since we'd left Fort Lauderdale and we were beginning to understand that the girl in Punta Gorda had been absolutely right. You ran out of time very quickly on this coast: The hot old Caribbean sun roared up, you had breakfast, then it was time for bed.

I T HADN'T been the *Lord Jim*'s fault. The *Lord Jim* was fine, so fine that (as I've explained) a black reef of future trouble seemed to be building up ahead of us. All the systems were still go: The eighty-five-horse Perkins diesel started at the first touch of the key, ticking off the hours with a powerful chiming whine. The Magnavox SATNAV (satellite navigational system) reduced all kinds of difficult navigational problems to a matter of pushing the right buttons: *We always knew exactly where we were.* The Roberts autopilot kept the boat on course day and night. The forty-five-pound CQR plow (with 200 feet of chain rode) and the thirty-five-pound Danforth anchors had held firm in some very questionable harbors. The pressurized water system let us choose a cool or hot shower to start the day. The Lavac toilet never clogged (well, only once). The Shipmate propane stove turned out meal after delicious meal (not to ignore the cook). And the sails did what they were supposed to do on a motorsailor like the *Lord Jim:* steady the motion so you didn't roll in the chop but cut cleanly through it. Their other crucial function—a backup system for when the engine quit—had not even begun to be tested.

I remember how it felt to get back to the *Lord Jim* after our sojourn on the trail of Catherwood and Stephens, followed by Christmas and New Year's in Mexico with our four daughters: *rather scary.* Because after I'd climbed on board, smelt the special smell of the wheelhouse (engine oil, teak oil, mildew, canvas, a touch of diesel smoke), touched the varnished wheel, sensed the sturdy bulk of the boat under me, I realized I loved her.

W E HAD held up all right ourselves, although during the holiday season in Mexico, I'd noticed a small, painful lump under my scalp on the top of my head. It had grown to the size of about half a golf ball, with occasional twinges of hot, electric agony, before I told people about it.

The eggs of the botfly, common in Belize, are carried by a mosquito and transmitted when it bites. The eggs hatch into a grub which burrows into the living flesh of the host and feeds on it (painfully) until mature. Then it drops out of the host's flesh onto the ground, and metamorphoses into an adult fly. The hosts are commonly (but not limited to) cattle and wild animals. I had reason to believe I was a host.

Susan, a former physician's assistant who is used to hypochondria, always pooh-poohs my ailments. "What you have is a sebaceous cyst," she said smartly in front of all the daughters. "If you would just wash your hair more often . . ."

"*Yeah, Daddy.*"

She never learns, even after my wrist turned out to be really broken, or that I really did have serious aftereffects of "the bends." Or that . . .

Anyway, to make a long story short, when we got back to the Mañana Marina from Mexico I asked her to shave the golf-ball-sized lump and look at it closely.

"*Oh, gross. It goes in and out.*"

I asked her to explain calmly and clearly. When she'd touched the lump, something whitish and fairly large had disappeared into my head, leaving a hole.

ONE BOOK we read, *Backpacking in Central America*, said that lonely hikers frequently became attached to their worms and treated them as pets. That was a bit much. We tried to kill it by taping a wad of Cuban cigar tobacco over the breathing hole, as the book recommended, but each morning when Susan inspected it she would say the same thing:

"*God . . . look at it go in and out.*" It got old.

I thought she was beginning to hate me and my worm, the pus that dribbled out of the breathing hole, and my incessant complaining. Plus, I couldn't shake the cold I'd caught in Mexico: It had gotten to the green snot stage, and there was a lot of hawking and spitting during the day and snoring at night. I was turning into an object of disgust. I'd catch her watching me sometimes with a look I knew from past occasions in our sailing career. It meant she might be about to jump ship.

But Somebody was watching out for us. One morning, after another session of the usual, I came on deck to see the Frenchman on the next boat was wearing a truly arresting T-shirt. On his chest was a big red circle with a line drawn diagonally across it. Under the line was a yellow grub that looked quite a bit like what Susan had been describing.

Wormbusters.

Our common language was Spanish. "Excuse me," I said, pointing at the grub on his chest. "I think I have one of those." I pointed at my head. "Here."

"*Alors . . .*"

I took off the hat that Susan had been making me wear. His fingers probed and pushed in a wonderfully capable manner. There was a hissing intake of breath. "*Sí. Colmoyote.*"

The Frenchman turned out to be a veterinarian, the in-country administrator of an international aid program called "Veterinarians Without Frontiers." His Guatemalan assistant happened to be on board, helping him work on the boat. They couldn't begin to count how many *colmoyotes* (as botfly larvae are called in Guatemala) they had taken from cattle, but they'd never before had the chance to take one from a human being.

The two of them excitedly washed their hands. I sat down on a stool and all the Mañana Marina people gathered around. I suggested that Susan get a photograph, but she wouldn't.

The assistant squeezed on the golf-ball-sized lump with his thumbs while the vet pulled gently. It seemed to take forever. In the end there was a gasp of relief from the gathered crowd and the vet laid an object the size of a .38 caliber pistol bullet in the palm of my hand. The crowd cheered. The thing had two hooks on one end, five rings of black bristles, and lived in alcohol for half an hour afterward.

MY COLD had cleared up and Susan had stayed. She herself had been doing better than just "holding up," in fact. Seven months before we set sail she'd ruptured two discs in her back, had been immobilized for two weeks, and had lost some function in her foot. Now she could raise anchors, lower sails, and cause heads to turn in any main street in Central America.

Boat life was better than Elizabeth Arden. *"You weren't really going to jump ship, were you?"*

"Probably not," she answered, with a hint of that same look. It's one of the things I like about her: that edge. But a few nights later, after a drunken dinner at Susanna's Restaurant celebrating our imminent departure from the Mañana Marina, I pushed her overboard.

The only way to get to Susanna's is by boat; we had a little inflatable with an eight-horsepower outboard which with only two people could get up on a plane and go along at a respectable rate of speed. It was fun sometimes to bounce along the tops of the waves—at least I thought so.

But for the past few years, since first my daughter and then I drove my car off the road with Susan in the passenger seat, she has been more and more uneasy with speed. I'd call it a phobia.

A psychiatrist friend explained it this way: *Susan feels as if she'd like to be more in control. Speed, when she's not driving, has become a direct threat to her authority.*

The Argentinian mechanic who works on my fast little car put it like this: *Women hate these cars; they want to take them away just like they'd like to cut off your balls.*

All I know for sure is that when I first got the car I could go 120 with no complaints. Now I'm lucky if I can get over 70. Long trips have turned into a grim contest of wills. To me, speed is freedom.

So here we were, drunk and happy, coming back from our goodbye dinner in our little inflatable at about midnight. The Río Dulce was glassy and reflected the stars, but it was really very dark and we had no flashlight. I gunned the engine to get the boat planing and the waves of rage coming from Susan's side were worse than Tropical Storm Karen.

"Do we have to do this?"

"Do you want to spend an hour getting back?"

We sped along gaily in the darkness, feeling as if we were speeding along in outer space with no connection to anything. Even the waves of rage. The lights of the Mañana Marina and their exactly symmetrical reflections grew larger and more beautiful. But Susan was screaming:

"I can't take it anymore. Slow down!"

Things became very calm and logical. The lights of the marina were now close, only about 100 yards away. The water was warm, clean, and fresh. I knew there were no dangerous fish around. I thought: She's probably never been pushed overboard before; I planted the palm of my hand suddenly on her breastbone. There was the sight of feet in the air and a nice splash. I thought: She's probably going to come up laughing.

As soon as I was able to stop laughing myself, I turned back to pick her up. She said she would rather swim, and for a while I continued to hope that she was in fact enjoying the experience.

F ROM SUSAN'S personal log:

The night before we left the Mañana Marina we went to Susanna's Restaurant. He'd already had *two hard liquor* drinks at the Mañana. At Susanna's he had four large glasses of wine.

We dinghied across the bay home slapping into the waves. I *hate* going fast and Gordon is very familiar with that. As we neared the boat I asked him to *please* slow down since we were almost there. He said no. I threw the flashlight onto the dinghy floor. He threw me overboard. Two acts of abusive, violent behavior in two weeks *which* I have accepted. I am very ashamed I haven't jumped ship, but I really want to do this trip and if that's the trade-off, I'll accept it. Another instance of cruelty will be the last . . .

There had been silence all the way to Honduras. She told me there how close she'd been to jumping ship for good.

I'd been more worried about that possibility than I wanted to admit. Because I'd come to realize at this late date that there was no way I'd be able to go on without her. But that was only *after* I'd pushed her overboard.

FINALLY THE winter weather had caught up with us. As soon as we'd left Guatemala we began to feel what we'd expected all along: the heavy hand of the Northeast Trades on our nose. This was the coast that Columbus named *Honduras,* meaning deep, because the huge waves and high winds had seemed like open ocean. And we began to understand how his Fourth Voyage through here turned out to be his last, and exactly why he had named the easternmost cape Cabo Gracias a Dios: Thanks be to God.

The name of the game was shelter. On the long beat east to Trujillo we hopped from harbor to harbor, never going more than thirty miles a leg and usually sailing after midnight because that's when the wind was lightest. And some of the roughest weather we encountered was in the Nicaraguan Embassy in Tegucigalpa, negotiating for the first visa granted to an American "pleasure craft" since the Sandinistas took office, to sail down the country's strategically flaky Caribbean coast. Actually, the first letters of our application had been written months before by "Sandalista" contacts ... these being the long-haired, Birkenstocked gringo supporters of the revolution who over the years have turned out to be former college roommates, relatives, colleagues, and love objects.

I N ONE of these mostly uninspiring harbors—possibly Puerto Cortés, listening in my sleep to the midnight sound of U.S. Marines offloading their equipment from the USS *Barnstable County*—I dreamed I had finally graduated from St. Paul's, the fancy prep school I had been an unhappy inmate of for five endless years. A square peg in a round hole ... and a *little* square peg at that: My voice hadn't even begun to change until I was seventeen. The lessons I learned at St. Paul's had much more to do with being the object of humiliation than with gracefully joining the ruling classes.

Was it possible? In this dream we were all more or less the same size, standing in line to be called in one by one to the "graduation room."

My turn came, and I stepped through the door with some misgivings. But a panel of dignitaries congratulated me, and a Celtic-looking guy with bushy eyebrows and heavy eyelids handed me an Academy Award.

It was all too much. I burst into tears and asked him who he was. He just smiled, and I saw he was the editor who had turned down my novel the year before.

All this by way of reaffirming (I guess) that boat life is good for you. At least, I was glad to be given the Academy Award by that formerly skeptical editor; the graduation part I'm not so sure about.

WILL PORTER (he had taken the pen name O. Henry from a guard at the penitentiary where he served three years for embezzling) was a little more than thirty when he came to Trujillo in the mid-1890s fleeing those same charges. He was small, sickly, and nondescript . . . a perfect bank teller or drugstore clerk, which is how he'd made his living up to then in Austin, Texas. Plus, of course, the embezzling—a little under $1,000—and a weekly humor sheet called *Rolling Stone* that lasted for less than a year. He had never done any real writing, other than some scribbling for the magazine. Trujillo was his inspiration.

In those days Trujillo was the main port into northern Central America; this was when Americans, having disposed of their own frontier and desperately needing another, were fantasizing the region as a place of "untapped potential." The banana business was just getting under way and . . . there was no government! If there was, it could be bought for a nickel. Or changed.

It was all wide open. Every floater and opportunist in the hemisphere had either passed through or was actually living there. *"There is an American colony,"* says one character in *Cabbages and Kings,* O. Henry's comic opera of all these doings . . . also his first and only book. *"Some of the members are all right. Some are fugitives from justice from the States. I recall two exiled bank presidents, one army paymaster under a cloud, a couple of manslayers, and a widow—arsenic, I believe, was the suspicion in her case . . ."*

TRUE TO the Mosquito Shore format in general, the look of things hasn't changed much in Trujillo for the past 100 years. And it was indeed a calm, idyllic morning (one of the few)

as we motored across the wide glassy bay toward the historic little cluster of white houses under the high green mountains. *The waves swished along the smooth beach; the parrots screamed in the orange and ceiba trees; the palms waved their limber fronds foolishly like an awkward chorus at the prima donna's cue to enter...*

We rowed ashore in the inflatable (I'd agreed not to use the motor for a while) and saw that the old banana pier where Will Porter himself must have landed was now too rickety for comfort. We pulled the inflatable up on the little beach at the foot of the pier under the eyes of a young tourist couple in straw hats and cameras and tried to ignore them.

"Nice boat," the guy said. It helped a little, but not much, to learn they were Peace Corps volunteers.

ONE OF the first people Will Porter met in Trujillo was a bank robber named Al Jennings, fresh off the New Orleans packet himself. According to Jennings's memoirs, they had the following conversation:

"Say, mister," I (Jennings) asked, "could you lead me to a drink. Burnt out on Three Star Hennessey. Got a different brand?"

"We have a lotion here that is guaranteed to uplift the spirit," he answered in a hushed undertone that seemed to charge his words with vast importance.

"Are you the American consul?" I ventured, also in a whisper.

"No, just anchored here," he smuggled back the information. Then his cool glance rested on the ragged edge of my coat.

"What caused you to leave in such a hurry?" he asked.

"Perhaps the same reason that routed yourself," I retorted.

The merest flicker of a smile touched his lips. He got up,

took my arm, and together we helped each other down the street, that was narrow as a burrow path, to the nearest cantina.

Several hours we sat there, an ex-highwayman in a tattered dress suit and a fugitive in spotless white ducks, together planning a suitable investment for my stolen funds. Porter suggested a coconut plantation, a campaign for the presidency, an indigo concession . . .

The Peace Corps couple volunteered to show us the sights, and were taken aback to learn we had no interest in the place where Columbus had the first mass celebrated on the American continent in 1502. Or the place where Cortés proclaimed it Spanish territory in 1524. Or the old Spanish fort that Henry Morgan plundered in 1665. Or the place where William Walker was shot in 1860. Or the old headquarters of the legendary mercenary Lee Christmas, who launched a revolution here in 1911 for Sam (the Banana Man) Zemurray (a Founding Father of United Fruit) and later had himself proclaimed commander-in-chief of the Honduran Army.

"No, no," we said. "We're O. Henry fans. We want to see where he lived."

O. Henry's former residence was not on the regular tour route. The Peace Corps couple told us we might be able to get some information at the museum. And even if we couldn't, the museum was worth visiting in itself.

I felt like saying: "We didn't sail a thousand miles to the Mosquito Shore so we could go to a museum."

"This one's different." Had he read my mind?

WE WALKED through town. Due to centuries of plundering and fires there were very few buildings that looked older than the standard Victorian bungalow.

The side streets were covered by a growth of thick, rank grass, which was kept to a navigable shortness by the machetes of the police. Stone sidewalks, little more than a ledge in width, ran along the base of the mean and monotonous adobe houses ... A few structures raised their heads above the red-tiled roofs— the bell tower of the Calaboza, the Hotel de los Estranjeros, the residence of the Vesuvius Fruit Company's agent, the store and residence of Bernard Brannigan, a ruined cathedral in which Columbus had once set foot, and, most important of all, the Casa Morena—the summer "White House" of the President. On the principal street along the beach—the Broadway of Coralio—were the larger stores, the government bodega and the post office, the cuartel, the rum shops and the market place. (From *Cabbages and Kings*)

Now the cathedral had been repaired ... although one has to doubt whether Columbus ever set foot in it; when he showed up the only inhabitants were Indians who did not believe in God or build cathedrals. And the *Calaboza* (the jail) had a new sign: LA LEY ES DURO, PERO ES LA LEY (the law is hard, but it is the law). The rank grass was still there, but the "Vesuvius Fruit Company" (aka United Fruit) and the "Summer White House" were long gone, and so was the store and residence of "Bernard Brannigan," the generic *"small adventurer, with empty pockets to fill, light of heart, busy-brained—the modern fairy prince, bearing an alarm clock, more surely than by the sentimental kiss, to awaken the beautiful tropics from the centuries' sleep."*

The Peace Corps couple were about the only small adventurers left. Do-gooders had replaced the desperadoes. The hot old cobblestoned streets that had seen so much questionable history were finally quiet, peaceful, and boring.

Even the old graveyard looked less haunted by antiquity than just run-down. William Walker, the quintessential American adventurer who conquered and proclaimed himself president of Nicaragua in 1856, had been buried here after his execution at the fort. His grave, a simple headstone reading WILLIAM WALKER

1860 and surrounded by a wrought-iron fence, was distinguished by a beaten path in the knee-high grass that covered the rest of the area. And we had to wonder who it was that had beaten out the path.

T HE MUSEUM was on the outskirts of town, in a grove of trees next to a waterfall and a deep clear pool. A little spa had been built around the pool—tables, chairs, even a tiny suspension bridge—there were walkways through the trees with more tables and chairs. It was all made from old auto parts and other junk, brightly painted in yellows, blues, and reds. Birdsong echoed through the huge trees, light slanted down in dusty bars . . . the place was deserted.

Up through the trees we could see a big, metal-roofed shed; in front of it was an ancient Caterpillar tractor and the quite modern wreckage of an airplane. The door was opened by a short, heavily breathing bald man with thick glasses, black shoes with the laces untied, and a T-shirt that said CASINO ROYAL. He said he owned the museum and his name was Rufino Galán.

We pointed at the wreckage. "Very interesting."

He seemed to swell a little in size. "Yes, señor. Brought by United States soldiers. On a truck."

It was his prize exhibit, a C-130 Hercules troop transport that had crashed in the ocean off Trujillo January 22, 1985, killing all twenty-one United States Air Force personnel on board. Inside the shed was what could only be called a shrine: twenty-one polished brass name plaques arranged in a semicircle with a little American flag under each. In the far bend of the semicircle were framed letters from Michael Dukakis and Ted Kennedy (some of the servicemen had come from Massachusetts). There were pictures of all the men. And there was a big plaque from the father of one inscribed: TO RUFINO GALÁN AND

THE PEOPLE OF TRUJILLO FROM WILLIAM R. ROBINSON. FOR HONOR AND THE UNITED STATES.

Every year, Señor Galán said, there was a mass celebrated at the museum in honor of the dead men. Last year 100 townspeople came.

It was far from the only exhibit. The museum was obviously the lifework of an energetic man.

S EÑOR GALÁN was sixty. His father had grown bananas for United Fruit a few years after O. Henry's time. Señor Galán had grown up in Trujillo but as a young man somehow had managed to spend a year in New York. It changed his life:

"I went to the museums there, and I'm going to tell you what I saw in them. Things from here. Important things. You see, all our best things are in museums in New York." Señor Galán decided his mission was to start a museum in which Honduras's heritage would be preserved at home.

There is an ancient telephone, from the United Fruit Company office. A United Fruit Company ventilator and water heater. Old United Fruit banana bags hanging from the ceiling. A Zenith Transoceanic radio, circa 1950. A Blaupunkt high-fidelity system from the same era. Other old radios. A foot-operated Singer sewing machine. A lawnmower. Various pieces of furniture. "All United Fruit. The tractor outside, also." Many items have the names and addresses of their former owners, and quite a few of the names are English. In a glass case is a copy of the *processo* of William Walker, his last statement.

"Many things from America," I smiled at him. "Here in Honduras."

"*Claro.*"

"There was an American writer called O. Henry (in Spanish, this came out *Ojenri*) who lived here a long time ago. Do you know about him?"

"*Claro que sí, señor.*"

"Do you have anything of his here?"

"He was an *American* writer, no?"

"Yes."

"Then he must have used a machine." Señor Galán took us to a huge collection of old typewriters. "One of these was his."

There seemed to be hundreds of them . . . mostly Royals. "They look too new," I said doubtfully. "Did they *use* typewriters in 1890?"

"*Claro* . . . you should know, señor. It was invented by Americans, no?"

"Maybe it was."

"Yes, it was, señor. And the airplane, the light bulb, the telephone, the electric chair . . ."

"Okay . . . but how do you know one of these was O. Henry's?"

"He was a writer, no? I have them all . . . every old typewriter in Trujillo. If he wrote a word on one of them, it is here."

Looking around, you could see that it was true: He had them all. "It is amazing," I said. "What you have here is truly amazing."

"*Claro,*" he said sadly. "But you are probably the last people who will see them. I'm going to close."

We stood there in amazement. "But all these things . . . what will happen to them?"

He shook his head and shrugged.

"But why?"

"There are never any tourists here. There is no attempt to get them . . . the tourist bureau in Tegucigalpa, they are not interested. Nobody is interested here. When the tourists come

113

they just raise their prices and drive them away. They don't appreciate them."

"That's a shame. But the museum is for Hondurans, no?"

Señor Galán just laughed. "And something else," he said, pointing at the deserted spa. "The mayor now says he wants to charge me for the water."

He was a proud man, obviously. A sign on the wall of the shed read in English: WE JUST ASK FOR RESPECT AND MORAL. THANK YOU.

SEÑOR GALÁN had shown us on an old aerial photograph of the house where he thought O. Henry had lived . . . he said the house had been adobe and was now in ruins. It had been right across the street from the cathedral, half a block from the main square, and only a few hundred yards from the fort. Nicely situated, as they used to say. Of course at the time, Will Porter was almost $1,000 to the good.

All that was left were the thick adobe walls and a kind of enclosed, brick-paved courtyard. The adjoining adobe house was also ruined, so the only neighbor was the house that abutted on the back and faced on the main street, the "Broadway of Coralio." It was now a restaurant. A young man was going through the accounts when we walked in, but it was too early for diners.

When we told him we were interested in the old house in back, he went and got his mother.

She was not old—fiftyish—a no-nonsense lady with her hair in a tight bun. "Do you want to buy it?"

"No, no."

"Because these old houses are increasing in value. Many Americans are buying them."

"But it's all fallen down. There's nothing there."

"They are easy to fix up. The foundations are very strong."

"We will have to think about it," I said politely. "But we wanted to talk to you about an American who lived there a long time ago, in 1890. A writer named O. Henry."

She was losing interest. "Well then you should talk to Señor Galán at the *museo*. He's the only one that knows about those things from the old days, the old gringo things."

"There's no one else?"

"No one, señor. Can't you see? But we are still here, aren't we? Even so."

BACK DOWN at the old banana pier the skipper of the *Soto Calypso,* which had brought a cargo of fish and lobsters from Grand Cayman and was going back with fruit, had some bad news. A strong cold front was due in the next day and the anchorage at Trujillo was unprotected. He was going across the big bay to Puerto Castilla. He was an attractive Ladino who had been spending a good part of each day in the ship's hammock with a series of beautiful *Trujillanas,* but he was so busy getting his boat ready he didn't have time to smile at the two who were watching from the pier. We decided to go too.

The anchorage at Puerto Castilla was protected from the north, but that was all. And to get any real protection even from the north, you had to anchor in uncomfortably shallow water . . . less than eight feet . . . where the chop could start to break if it got too big. We put out our big CQR plow anchor and about fifty feet of chain and sat in the dark wheelhouse listening to the rising wind and watching the lights of the coastal traders and fishing boats come straggling in. Farther west, opposite the big new pier there were even some larger freighters. We rolled into our snug bunk in the forepeak and were cocky enough ourselves to get a good night's sleep in spite of the snapping of the flags.

A T DAWN things didn't look too bad. The wind was barely twenty knots off the land and the chop was easy. The *Soto Calypso* was a few hundred feet to the west . . . the captain waved at us from the bow, where he was checking his anchor. We waved back, went below and fixed ourselves a big breakfast. We didn't quite get to the point of congratulating ourselves.

At ten o'clock we moved the *Lord Jim* farther east into what seemed more protected water, because the chop where we were had steepened and was beginning to break on us. The wind had risen to about thirty knots and shifted northwest, so there was less shelter. The *Soto Calypso* followed us.

At about noon, we moved the *Lord Jim* as close to the shore as we thought we could get. The *Soto Calypso* followed. The wind was about forty knots: It had stopped howling in the rigging and was beginning to shriek. You couldn't say the rain was falling anymore either; it was moving at you horizontally like a charge of buckshot. The chop was about five feet and breaking routinely in the shallow water . . . our broad bouyant bow lifted nicely over the larger rollers.

Susan maneuvered while I sat on the bow and divided the universe of wind, rain, and spume with my face. I dropped the Danforth and then the CQR so the two anchor rodes led back to the boat at an angle of about twenty degrees. After we had swung into position we saw we were directly downwind from a large shrimp boat called *The Gulf Queen*. Susan's watch has a date-meter and she noticed that it was February 25, Election Day in Nicaragua.

I SHOULD SAY here that all the windspeed estimates are strictly off the top of my head. Maybe they are more or less equivalent to the size of the fish that got away. Who can be sure? I do know, though, that some of the sailing books in our library have pictures and descriptions of the ocean at various windspeeds. When the wind began blowing the tops off the waves and the flying spume lowered the visibility to about fifty feet, we figured it was about Force 9 on the Beaufort scale, "a strong gale, 47–54 miles per hour." Well, it felt like a hurricane.

Boats were beginning to break loose from their anchors, or the anchors were dragging. The *Soto Calypso* captain got his up and motored out of sight into the murk. The boat next to us was hit by a drifting fishing smack (we could hear things snapping and breaking even over the wind) and both of them disappeared astern, locked in a costly and possibly final embrace.

I looked at the seventy-foot *Gulf Queen* plunging scarily upwind from us and thought: *Susan says she's fine as long as she knows what to expect.* A good thought under the circumstances, because the next one had to be: *What should we expect?*

Susan fixed two cups of coffee while I warmed the engine up and got the anchor rodes ready to jettison. It was all part of the plan. We stood in the wheelhouse drinking the coffee and saw— *just as we expected*—the *Gulf Queen* break loose and begin to drift down on us. The precise path she would take was still not clear.

It was all part of the plan: We needed, of course, to get out of her way before she smashed us to kindling. But there was the problem of our two anchors. The plan was that Susan would maneuver the *Lord Jim* out of the way while I paid out the anchor rodes as far as they'd go and cast them loose if that wasn't far enough. I handed her my coffee cup and got ready to run up on the bow. She took the coffee cups down to the galley . . .

"Susan! Jesus Christ, what are you doing?"

"We have plenty of time. Just go on up."

I was gone. In a few minutes, I could feel what I hoped were the right ropes under my hands. I began to let out scope while the *Lord Jim* seemed to be inching over to starboard. The question was: How far was far enough? From my envelope of elements I could barely see Susan's face in the wheelhouse window, much less the *Gulf Queen*. It was out of my hands. I didn't have to do anything but hang on while the *Gulf Queen* swept past about fifteen feet to port.

When she had disappeared astern I stripped off my soaked clothes, went down to the galley, and got the coffee. I drank mine in two gulps and began to shake so hard I had to sit down.

Susan was calm and smiling. And the sequence completed itself with this final thought: *Who in God's name am I traveling with?*

I N THE late afternoon, the wind began to drop and by dusk the storm was history. I felt like I had to get off the *Lord Jim* for a little while; Susan wanted to stay aboard. I rowed ashore and walked across the narrow neck of land that separates Puerto Castilla from the ocean.

A kid was standing in the dunes next to a big olive-drab Chevy Blazer.

"Quite a storm, wasn't it?" I said to him in Spanish.

"*No entiendo.*" He didn't understand. And he had an American accent.

"You're an American," I said stupidly. "Me too."

He seemed nervous about something. Maybe I didn't really look like an American. After all, I had just been through the worst storm of my life at sea . . . maybe I had the "10,000-mile stare" as they used to call it in Vietnam.

He kept looking over his shoulder. The storm surf on the big ocean beach was spectacular, as if the ocean was somehow avalanching down from the horizon. And I began to see that the surf was full of naked men, running and jumping in the waves. They looked in excellent shape.

They were United States Marines, from "one of the airbases" in southern Honduras near the Nicaraguan border, in Trujillo on a school-building project. The kid had been posted as a sentry. "We just drove over to see the waves," he explained with an embarrassed grin and—I swear to God—a blush. And here we both were in Honduras.

"Well . . . take it easy," I said.

"You too."

I walked away down the loud, darkening beach, thinking about love, and who I was traveling with, and as usual didn't come up with any answers.

D ANIEL ORTEGA had lost the Nicaraguan election, we learned the next day. Now what? After all, his administration had been enlightened enough to grant our visa applications . . . even during the critical election period. In fact, he had had the balls to allow hundreds of foreign observers in, and to have the first free election in the history of Nicaragua. You had to respect him, even if he had been cocksure of winning.

We had to think what it all meant for us. The Sandinistas weren't due to turn over the government for two more months, so we would be dealing with a lame-duck administration that would no doubt hate the United States for its shameless backing of the opposition candidate, Violeta Chamorro. Of course, it was entirely possible that Ortega might decide to stay . . .

Either way prospects didn't look good, and we still had a lot of tricky ground to cover before we even got there: the Mosquito Coast of Honduras . . . from the nautical aspect, maybe the trickiest ground.

East of Trujillo, the coastal mountains peter out in a virtually trackless system of swamps, rivers, lagoons, and pine barrens. The harbors are all dangerously shallow inlets, directly exposed to the trades. The Spanish had tried once or twice to colonize it, but in the end had left it to the English and a strange race of hybrids called Miskito Indians who were their creations and from whom the coast took its name.

On the arrival of the first Europeans, the Miskito Indians were as purebred as the other tribes but with one important cultural difference. The women were ready and willing to take the Europeans (English buccaneers, mostly) as husbands, if only for an hour or two. There was no stigma on the child, which was considered Miskito. So while the other tribes were cut down by disease and bullets, the Miskitos flourished and looked less and less like Indians.

Europeans or Africans: It didn't really matter. When a Portuguese slave ship (commanded by the slaves, who had killed the captain and crew) was wrecked south of Cabo Gracias a Dios, the slaves quickly became part of the tribe. The Spanish named the resulting subgroup Zambos (probably from *ambos,* meaning both) which became Sambo in English . . . as in "Little Black Sambo."

Miskitos just want to have fun. Orlando Roberts, a sober, levelheaded coastal trader in the early nineteenth century, was scandalized at one typical bacchanale:

> The drinking was carried on with great perseverance, during the night, by old and young. The drums were beat, and muskets fired, some of them loaded with powder to the very muzzle, until nearly all the assembly were in a state of beastly drunkenness, and taken care of by the women, who were

occasionally called upon for that purpose. At intervals, however, as the men recovered, they found their way back to their favorite mishlaw, and renewed the debauch. All the next day was consumed in drinking; and, it was not until the day following, that the liquors were reduced to the very dregs of the cassava and maize, which, even then, was taken from the bottom of the vessels, and being squeezed through the fingers, by handfuls, into the calabashes, was passed to those who were still craving for more of the precious beverage. By the third night, the whole liquors were consumed; and the Indians began to retire to their respective homes, many complaining, with great reason, that "their heads were all spoiled."

The Miskitos, being the seedy, fun-loving folk that they were, traditionally allied themselves with the British buccaneers against the straightlaced Catholic Spaniards. In 1687, the British formalized the arrangement by shipping the Sambo chief to Jamaica, dressing him up in a "cocked hat", red coat, shirt, and broadsword, presenting him with a certificate, and crowning him King of Mosquitia with a typical British feeling for pomp. The Miskitos loved it and the system continued almost without break well into the nineteenth century, when Britain agreed to withdraw from the Shore.

Strangely enough—or maybe not so strangely—I identified with the Miskitos.

Two hundred years of separatism does not disappear overnight . . . as the Sandinistas were to discover. When they first took over in 1979 they hailed the neglected Miskitos as brothers-in-revolution . . . actually the Miskitos liked Somoza because he had let them alone.

The Sandinistas heralded the Atlantic coast as Nicaragua's New Frontier. They nationalized the area's gold mines, fishing cooperatives, and lumber concessions; developed special bilingual education programs for the English-speaking Miskitos; and created a political organization (MISURASATA) to represent them in Managua. A year later they had decided the Miskitos were a threat to the revolution and began burning down their villages. Some 30,000 Miskitos fled across the border into Honduras, and quite a few of those thousands joined the Contras or began their own guerrilla operations. Or both.

W E WANTED to ride the last of the storm wind east, but the ocean was still too rough for safe entrance through the inlets so we had to spend the next day in port. Drizzle and gray skies: a good day for sleeping late, reading, and phone calls on the single-side-band. Radio Martí, the Voice of America propaganda station beamed at Cuba, was playing a good selection of Golden Oldies: Rita Coolidge, Elton John, Olivia Newton-John.

I had brought along my father's copy of William Albert Robinson's *Deep Water and Shoal* (1932), in which the young author drops out and sails around the world in a twenty-seven-foot ketch . . . at the time the smallest vessel ever to do so.

> I have been asked to introduce Mr. William Robinson's book to British readers; but I hesitate to do so, because I have to remember it is the fate of the majority of British readers to have to catch the 9.15 three hundred times each year, and I think this book will make every season-ticket holder who reads it very restless and discontented with his life. (Weston Martyr, London, 1932)

In 1932 my father was a shipping clerk in Calcutta, India . . . a *square peg in a round hole.* Like me, he had been a shrimp in boarding school . . . like me, he had done badly—so badly the headmaster had told his mother "forget about university." Oxford, where his father had gone and his brothers were to go to Sandhurst to begin their military careers (ending in death for his father in Belgium in World War I, and for his youngest brother in North Africa in World War II) was out of the question. The question then became "What to do with young Charles . . . a bit of a problem." I was familiar with a similar question.

His mother's new husband was a stockbroker . . . one of his clients happened to own a shipping company with offices in Calcutta, then part of the British Empire. So it goes.

So here was my father, a season-ticket holder on the 9:15 to the Port of Calcutta. Things were closing in: The owner of the company had lost a shooting match to my step-grandfather and in a huff had withdrawn his entire account . . . my father suddenly found himself on a very slow track with no prospect of advancement. He'd enjoyed recreational flying in the company's De-Havilland Tiger Moth biplane, but had crashed—pinning his immediate superior in the wreckage—and his license to fly in India had been pulled forever. Not too long after *Deep Water and Shoal* made it to Calcutta, my father and a friend were on a packet back to London, where they bought a twenty-year-old squaresail yawl and outfitted her to follow in Robinson's wake all the way to Tahiti, a place "inhabited by men who came for a vacation and stayed forever" where Robinson himself had dropped anchor for good. My father was twenty-seven. He got as far as the West Indies, at least, before he met my uncle, Cummins Catherwood . . . who introduced him to my mother.

To me it was the eve of the Great Adventure. Everything else had been mere preparation. The real thing lay ahead, and I was anxious to be off. I live my life like that—looking always to what lies ahead. Some time later, perhaps, I will live in the present. When I am old I will have my past, and if that past measures up at all to the future I dream of now, my life will have been complete . . .

Heady stuff, all right. I read *Deep Water and Shoal* for a few hours and then happened to notice it had been inscribed: *"To*

*Charles Chaplin, with best wishes . . . William Albert Robinson,
Tahiti, 1976.''* The old blade finally had made it to Tahiti . . . a
seventy-year-old passenger on the cruise ship *Sagafjord.* By that
time it was the only way my mother could travel comfortably. I
knew that part already. But typically he had never told me about
taking the book along and tracking Robinson down after all those
years for the inscription. And I'll lay odds he never told Robinson
about his own trip.

R ECEPTION ON the single-side-band was not too good that
day. And the old blade's ears were getting worse all the
time. "Just a minute," said my stepmother doubtfully. "I'll put
him on, but I'm not sure he'll be able to hear you."

"Well, we made it through the storm all right," I said into
the microphone.

I could hear his British accent coming through, talking
about the weather in Nokomis, Florida, where they were spending the winter, and his plans to buy a little outboard runabout for
the lakes.

He wasn't getting it. I took a deep breath and shouted
across the skywaves: *"I'm kind of proud of myself."*

D RINKING OUR 100-watt Honduran coffee in the sunny
morning, we felt optimistic and decided to try the 140-
mile trip east to Puerto Lempira (the closest feasible harbor)
while we still had the favorable storm wind. The surge seemed to
have subsided a little and the coffee was making us surer than
ever that we had no time to lose.

In a few minutes, raising the anchor, the anchor chain

snapped off the little paddle-wheel protruding from the hull that told us how fast we were going and how many miles we'd gone: The log was now defunct and navigation would be that much harder. A short half hour later, motoring out of Puerto Castilla, the V-belt to the alternator that charged the house batteries broke . . . no house current for lights. As we rounded the point into the open ocean it appeared the autopilot was on the fritz and we would have to steer manually the whole way. We set the two downwind jibs on their two poles and one of the pole fittings snapped off. We were left with the single jib.

Four mishaps in less than a hour. The *Lord Jim,* being the Germanically equipped ship that she was, had backup systems for the log and the alternator but still . . . was this the black reef at last?

We could go back to Puerto Castilla, but then we'd lose the favorable wind. The log and the jibboom were irreparable without new parts, and there was no guarantee that we could fix the autopilot. We'd lose time.

We'd go on, and damn the torpedoes. The sun set lower over the lumpy brown swells and we poured ourselves a little grog. Things didn't look too bad . . . almost good, in fact. The remaining storm clouds treated us to a real Central American sunset and the *Lord Jim* roared on merrily down the unusual wind: It was like being able to coast uphill.

A S SOON as it was good and dark, the wind shifted dead ahead and a series of gusty rain squalls came marching down on us. I wrestled the remaining pole off the jib and we rolled the sail up: Now it was just a hindrance. The surface of the ocean came to resemble the water in a huge bathtub which a child is splashing in all different directions.

It was barely eight P.M. We would be beating into the wind for the next fifty miles before the land began to fall away to the south. We wouldn't arrive off the inlet to Caratasca Lagoon until well after dawn. With a very karmic crash, the stainless-steel swimming ladder fell off the roof of the wheelhouse and rolled overboard.

That made five.

We decided to go with hour-and-a-half watches instead of our usual three-hour ones; sleep would be impossible anyway. And the manual steering would be pretty exhausting. Through the windows of the wheelhouse the breaking waves all around us looked like white teeth in a black open mouth.

In the middle of my watch, I checked the inflatable towing behind us; the line had worn through two strands and was working on the third. Number six? I spent some ill-defined period of time getting another line on it and fitting a polyethylene chafeguard ... and it occurred to me that if the whole performance could have been filmed by a camera mounted on the hull the boat would look stationary and I'd seem to be flying around it like a nautical Peter Pan.

A LONE IN the dark, one's thoughts jump around too. Suddenly I remembered that my mother had originally planned to call my sister and me Peter and Wendy, from the original *Peter Pan*. Someone talked her out of it, thank God.

But wasn't that quite shockingly romantic?

"I could have had anybody around here," she used to tell me. "But I picked your father." It must have been quite a shock, all right: The rich young orphan spurns her eligible Philadelphia suitors to marry a penniless English adventurer. Somebody lent them a little boat for their honeymoon and away they sailed ... possibly forever.

It turned out to be the last cruise they ever took together. Boat life didn't agree with my mother and my father ended up ashore, in Philadelphia. Their circle of friends included many of her former suitors.

Money talks . . . romance walks. Was that it? But maybe I'd been deluding myself that in a way I was taking this trip for the old blade, a kind of seagoing proxy: doing something he would have loved to have done himself if he'd been allowed to. I remembered now that he'd always liked the creature comforts: One of his recurring nightmares was of being dipped in something sticky.

I checked my watch. These thoughts had been good for an hour and ten minutes. Time to get Susan up.

WHATEVER GETS you through the night. On my next watch it was Radio Australia, with a fine selection of rock and roll from the early sixties . . . at least, that's how it seemed. Maybe they were Australian musicians playing late eighties numbers. Anyway it all put me in mind of my own honeymoon, to Southeast Asia in 1967.

When we passed through Australia my wife's pregnancy was just starting to show. "Sugar Shack" was all the rage. We went shopping together in Sydney and picked out her first maternity dress: yellow linen with a white collar and buttons down the front. We picked out her second in Melbourne: navy blue wool, with a dark green collar. In Rockhampton we picked out a blue-and-white striped maternity bathing suit for diving on the Great Barrier Reef. And in our little cabin on the dive boat we examined her new belly: It was high, hard, and slightly triangular (inverted) and made me more excited than I've ever been before or since.

R ADIO AUSTRALIA faded out; the earphones were making my ears ache anyway. There was a nasty little time while I toyed with the question: "What am I doing here?" until it completely lost its meaning. The secret became just letting your mind float. The danger was that then some song might drift in and be impossible to get out . . . not the whole song, just a snatch:

> Oh it ain't no use to sit and wonder why, babe,
> If'n you don't know by now.
> ???

Maybe the fiftieth time around, babe, I began to notice that the waves outside were becoming visible. The flashing light at Punta Patuca, which I'd been tracking off and on for the last half-hour, faded out like the morning star and the land finally began to fall off to the south.

O N THE new angle we could sail again, instead of just powering straight into those arbitrary lumpy brown waves. The coast, about five miles off, was a long strip of light-colored beach backed by dark jungle . . . no different at all from the coast of Columbus's time. *La Mosquitia*. But after all the landscapes I had passed through in the dark, there was a question in my mind about whether this one was any more real, and for what reason.

H ERE'S THE way things are with boats. First, never congratulate yourself too soon . . . and it's safer not to congratulate yourself at all. After the tiny moment we allowed ourselves on getting through the worst night so far, we found the inlet to Caratasca Lagoon impassable: Breaking surf stretched right across it and a couple of fishing boats were heaving and plunging at anchor outside the surfline.

But second: Just when you think you've taken all you can stand, it turns out to be not that bad. The prospect of another night in that sea was doing terrible things to us . . . *the horror* . . . until we decided to turn off the engine and heave to. We sheeted the jib in tight and set the helm slightly into the wind. *Qué milagro!* The *Lord Jim* rode the swells slowly and steadily, like a duck. We were moving at about two or three knots (impossible to tell exactly without a log), too close into the wind to be sailing free, yet with the sails full enough to steady her and keep her moving. We programmed a destination (a waypoint) for the SATNAV five miles off the inlet and reached out to sea for three hours (there were no obstructions). Then we reached back to the waypoint. And again . . . Columbus, Admiral of the Ocean Sea, had done a variation of this maneuver to make headway during the day, without the SATNAV, of course. But the easy, ducklike motion of the *Lord Jim* was astounding and gratifying and we set the alarm for three-hour intervals and slept gratefully between tacks. And when the sun went down again we turned on the lights, had dinner, and went back to bed. We thought: Hell, we can live like this indefinitely.

B UT THE next morning we thought we might have had enough. Too much of a good thing can get to even the most nautical folk . . . and we did have a drawing of the channel given us by a lobster boat captain in the Bay Islands: Leave the wreck thirty yards to port.

We paused just outside the surfline like a diver will pause on the end of the board before deciding to dive another day. The waves looked about four feet high in the channel . . . about half of them were breaking.

"Just tell me what to expect," Susan said calmly. So it was decided.

It happened just like I said: Wonders never cease. I put the bow straight into the channel and gave her half power. Susan watched the waves coming up and shouted which way to turn to keep them straight astern. The pointed stern divided the waves exactly as it was designed to. The keel touched hard once, twice (white water all around from the breaking waves), and then we were through. A man watching from the beach to see us wrecked finally turned and went back into the forest.

I opened a beer. We dropped anchor in calm water past a protecting point and went back to bed again, completely exhausted with the effort of not congratulating ourselves. Later, of course, we learned that the drawing had been wrong and that the real channel was on the other side of the wreck.

W E WOKE up in the early afternoon, slightly unsettled by the absolute motionlessness of the *Lord Jim*—after more than a week of storm surge. It was hot and completely quiet, unless you counted the buzzing of a fly or two; even that sounded summery and lazy. I thought: This is *not* congratulation, just a statement of fact. We made it.

The cut into the lagoon was broad and deep. *Cayucos* were pulled up on the beach under a grove of palm trees where we could see a little village of thatched huts. The lagoon itself looked like the Eastern Shore of Maryland's side of the Chesapeake Bay: calm, vegetable-colored water, low islands riding on their mirages in the distance. The white triangular sails of the *cayucos* doubled for the sails of the skipjacks and yachts of the Chesapeake, although as far as I knew we were only the second "pleasure craft" to come in here in recent memory ... not even Columbus had tried it.

We were soon aground, just like the Chesapeake, even though we were still following the lobster-boat captain's drawing of the channel. It was kind of nice: nothing to do but wait for guidance. The water was brackish, also like the Chesapeake, when we swam in it; the hot, still air was like the Chesapeake in summer. Boat life had beautified our bodies ... so when we made love it wasn't too much different than it had been nine years before in the Chesapeake at the end of our voyage from Key West and the beginning of our time together.

[Caratasca Lagoon] abounds in various sorts of fish of the finest description, particularly mullet, calapaner, snoak, cavellee, and also manatee; and it is the constant resort of immense quantities of ducks, widgeon, teal, and various aquatic birds ... The land in the vicinity consists almost entirely of extensive and beautiful savannahs, covered with the finest pasturage, and abounding in deer and other game ... There are few pine trees in Croata, but on the opposite, or land side, there are ridges containing timber as large as any on the coast; behind these ridges, to the westward, the savannahs are bounded by gently rising hills, whose summits are covered by the most luxuriant vegetation; and on the banks of the streams of the interior, there is excellent mahogany and cedar of the finest quality and largest size ... (Orlando Roberts: *Voyages and Excursions in Central America,* 1827)

Sometime later we saw a big cloud of black smoke on the landward shore of the lagoon about five miles away; it connected itself to a large white boat, headed in our direction apparently through the air. We watched as the blue air (complete with waves) became blue water and the boat came closer, marking its passage. We waved as it chugged on by, put on our clothes, backed off the mud bank, and retraced its route to Puerto Lempira. It was easy. And we felt, a little bit, as if we were entering the Promised Land.

But there was no sign of the "immense quantities" of waterfowl described by Roberts . . . just a few pelicans. And, in fact, when we got to the markets in Puerto Lempira, there was no sign of any kind of abundance at all . . . no oysters, crabs, eels, snook, mullet, or bass. It was all gone now, after 150 years of overfishing, as it was also gone out on the closer reefs. One of the most disturbing sights of the trip was the "day's catch" at Santa Fe, a Garifuna village ten miles west of Trujillo: No fish was longer than six inches.

P UERTO LEMPIRA was a graceful town on a low bluff with what looked like green lawns under huge old mango trees and the standard tin-roofed wooden bungalows painted in pastels. A long, rickety pier projected about 100 yards across the shallows to deeper water . . . the end did not appear to be connected to the beginning. At the base of the pier was what looked like an impossibly fancy restaurant built out over the water with people sitting at booths on the veranda. Punta was coming from the jukebox. In back of the town were rolling bare hills of savanna.

The pier was crowded with people getting in and out of *cayucos* . . . the buses of these parts . . . holding about twenty passengers, powered by a single-cylinder diesel. We anchored near the end of the pier and watched them closely for signs of debauch; after all, they were Miskitos.

Except in their copper-colored skin and black hair, they differ materially from the other Indian tribes of Central America.

They are tall, slim, bony and muscular, with thin noses and sharp features. In character they are bold, daring, adventurous, quarrelsome and self-assertive, frank and outspoken to each other or to strangers, fond of the sea and of ships and not particularly clever in the bush . . . (C. Napier Bell: *Tangweera: Life and Adventures among Gentle Savages*, 1899)

From a distance, a crowd of Miskitos looks like something by van Gogh . . . wonderfully matched, almost insanely lambent colors, glowing from the inside out. These are their clothes. They aren't any kind of traditional costume . . . just regular, amazingly colored clothes.

There was one Miskito on the pier with almost no clothes . . . a pair of cutoff jeans was it. His skin was panther-black, not copper, and every muscle he had was perfectly defined under it. He had a body that could have won prizes but his right knee was frozen at a fifteen-degree angle and his terrible limp made all the other perfection grotesque. It was more than grotesque . . . there was something Shakespearean about the way he dragged his leg down the long perspective. We were sure he'd taken a Nicaraguan bullet there. We rowed in to the base of the pier and when he waved at us we quickly waved back.

On shore, I noticed that Miskito women were the most beautiful I'd ever seen . . . until I remembered I'd noticed that in every new port. But they did have a fine air of no-nonsense insouciance about them as they floated up and down the streets like bright jungle birds, underlining the fact that Miskitos are matriarchal.

The restaurant turned out to be a lot more seedy than it had looked from the boat. It was called the *Yampus,* meaning "ashes" in Miskito, because it was built on the ashes of the old restaurant. It had a big dance floor. Across the street was another place called The Bunker, with an even bigger dance floor. The two buildings were by far the biggest buildings in town.

A Miskito boy who didn't seem to be looking for a handout

took us to the office of the *Capitania del Puerto* to check in. The *Capitania* was a thin, young Ladino with dark glasses and a white naval uniform; he seemed to be staring at us in a very sinister way. We sweated nervously while he asked us the same questions over and over and when he tried to get up to shake our hands, stumbled and fell back in his chair. We realized he was stone drunk. "Don't worry, be happy," he said with a beautiful sad smile that probably had broken even a few Miskito hearts.

We were looking for an Episcopalian monk named Brother Michael. When we met him a month earlier in Puerto Cortés, the drab Honduran shipping center, he'd been wearing a brown robe tied with a heavy rope, a skull cap, a white vestment over the robe emblazoned front and back with the red Cross of St. George, and sandals. He hadn't been carrying a staff. But, after my five years at St. Paul's—an Episcopal church school—I was always interested in whatever bizarre twists and turns the modern church might be taking.

We found him in a tiny one-room cabin labeled *Partida Nacional* . . . apparently a former campaign headquarters. He'd changed his robe for khaki pants and lost his skull cap, but still had the red-crossed vestment and the sandals. There were two cute Miskito kids with him, presumably getting "instruction."

"You're just in time," he said to us happily.

I N A flat calm the next morning (while a laughing group of van Gogh women and children played at catching nonexistent fish in the shallows) we moved the *Lord Jim* a quarter-mile east, off a smaller dock and buildings owned by MOPAWI, a "Christian" development organization for Honduran Miskitos that runs a string of jungle trading posts. The landing was easier and the MOPAWI people—young Hondurans, English, Americans,

Argentinians—were wonderfully nice. But when we mentioned Brother Michael there was a collective clearing of throats.

"What?"

"Oh, nothing . . ."

For "background" on the area and on Brother Michael they recommended we talk to the Catholic priest, Father John, who had been in La Mosquitia—both on the Nicaraguan and Honduran sides of the river—for twenty-six years. Was every gringo in town a missionary?

The Catholic compound was fancier than the Episcopalian one. There was a big church, a health clinic run by five Capuchin sisters, a school, comfortable residences for the two priests and the sisters. Father John Francis Samsa was sixtyish, with the hearty, abstracted, slightly severe look of a parochial school athletic coach.

THE BACKGROUND reminded me of certain towns in Thailand during the Vietnam War.

Before the Nicaraguan revolution, Puerto Lempira had been nothing. Then suddenly it had an airport with regularly scheduled flights daily, some forty relief agencies, 600 Honduran troops, at least four churches, and a motel . . .

There were also 30,000 Nicaraguan Miskitos to be ministered to. "The Sandinistas made a terrible mistake. Instead of adapting the revolution to the Indian, they tried to adapt the Indian to the revolution." And when the Miskitos left Nicaragua, Father John left with them. He has appeared on a PBS special with signed written accounts from villagers of Sandinista torture, shootings, and destruction.

Peace hit. Now, more than half of the refugees have returned to Nicaragua, the relief agencies and troops are beginning to thin out, and the town's hopelessly dislocated economy is once more dependent on the old standby: lobsters. They didn't even get to finish the road connecting Lempira to the rest of the country.

W E WERE talking on the shady back porch of the residence. Brother Michael, wearing his Cross of St. George vestment over khaki pants, happened to walk by on the street. He was moving fast and didn't notice us.

"Quite a character," I prompted gently.

Father John cleared his throat. We watched Brother Michael stride along in his sandals, but his whistling was too far away to make out.

Father John allowed as to how Brother Michael was not helping the Catholic Church's efforts in Puerto Lempira. People didn't really differentiate between Catholics and Episcopalians: Neither were Moravians, the German Protestant sect which sent the first missionaries to the shore in the late 1840s and was still the Miskito church of choice.

"I guess he's not exactly the image you might be comfortable with," I said.

Father John shook his head impatiently, but, one has to add, with some amusement. "Frankly no. And there are stories . . ."

"Stories . . ."

"Well, you can hear them from anybody. It's a small community."

"Right . . ."

"But some of the young boys' *parents* are not pleased with his ministry at all."

We nodded.

"In the baptism ceremony. Clothes have been removed."

We shook our heads.

"He travels by boat to one of his churches in something that frankly amounts to a G-string."

"..."

"And that robe ..."

"We've seen it."

"Well, it's *coarsely* woven. And they say that underneath it ... (Father John shook his head and smiled sadly). So in certain slants of light there at the altar he stands revealed in all his glory ..."

The thrust of it all was that if we were seen too much in Brother Michael's company certain avenues of communication in Puerto Lempira might be closed to us. So we didn't say he'd invited us to dinner at The Bunker.

W E WERE early and had a beer at the bar while we waited for Brother Michael, wondering whether we were doing the right thing. *Just in time for what?* He had mentioned an evening of "traditional Miskito dancing." But some of the MOPAWI people had mentioned in passing that he was "indiscriminately handing out birth-control devices."

As our eyes became accustomed to the gloom, we saw that what we had thought to be a dark shadow at the other end of the bar was actually the crippled, panther-skinned Miskito we'd seen on the pier. He saw us looking at him, got up, limped over, and stood behind us. We could feel the force of him standing there and didn't dare to turn. I desperately wanted to see if it was a bullet wound in his knee ... he was just too terrifically grotesque to face.

It seemed he expected us to buy him a beer, like some Shakespearean beggar.

Our policy was not to indulge barefaced begging ... only drunks and kids usually tried it anyway. But this was very different. I would have bought him the beer if I'd dared to face him, but

I was frozen. I felt small, white, out-of-place . . . I had no right to be there: Maybe I wasn't there at all. I looked at Susan for support and . . . confirmation . . . and she looked back. We didn't smile and we didn't speak. We just looked at each other.

After a long time, a silky black hand appeared on the bar beside me. In the hand was money: two green lempira bills. The bills were laid gently on the bar and the hand withdrew. I could feel the pressure behind me dissipate, as if the lid had been taken off a boiling pot. I turned. He was gone.

The handsome Miskito barmaid was giggling and shaking her head. The money sat there: I didn't touch it, she didn't touch it. When Brother Michael came in and waved us over to a table, I left it on the bar. Brother Michael said the man was known as *El Loco,* the crazy one, and had just appeared in Lempira recently. No one knew anything about him.

BROTHER MICHAEL was big and fit, in his early thirties. He had short brown hair (bald on top) and a slightly reptilian smile that Susan said was "deranged." But to me his eyes were surprisingly steady . . . and I noticed that people in The Bunker were hardly treating us like pariahs. I felt some kind of bond with him, I realized, that was a little unsettling in view of all that gossip. And, of course, in view of his calling. Why the Miskitos needed Episcopalianism and all its High-Church trappings was a question that I definitely wasn't equipped to answer in terms of my own experience.

I asked him how he happened to be an Episcopalian . . . he certainly didn't look like the ones I was used to.

He said his mother was English. When I told him my father was English and had sent me to an Episcopalian school where we had to go to church every day and twice on Sundays, he smiled and said: "That's not enough."

"What is enough?"

"*Seven* times a day." He was serious. But still, I felt this bond.

He had grown up near the port of Houston, Texas, where his father was a captain in the Merchant Marine. He'd graduated from Rice in 1979 with a degree in political science, and supported himself driving a delivery truck while he dabbled in local politics and church affairs. Then a friend told him about a dream in which he—Michael Thannisch Underhill—was a missionary surrounded by orphans.

"I was a delegate at the Republican Convention in Corpus Christi . . . after that was over, I just kept heading south." Evangelically speaking, it was all happening in Honduras.

He presented himself to the Episcopal Bishop of Honduras (a Cuban) as a layman, but said he wanted to do missionary work and to found his own order: of Joseph of Arimathea, the first missionary in the New Testament. "So far, I'm the only member . . . you need six to be recognized. But the bishop supports the order, and he's promised to ordain me a deacon soon."

Meanwhile, the bishop sent him to Lempira, where he said he had founded five churches in his five years of residency. Tomorrow was Sunday: We told him we'd love to come to at least one of them; Susan is an Episcopalian, too. He said the service would be in Miskito, and we enjoyed imagining the Miskito version of the Niceaen Creed and "Onward, Christian Soldiers."

THE "TRADITIONAL Miskito dancing" was to take place in the living room of a little house on pilings not too far from The Bunker. Brother Mike's vestment was a glimmer of white in the darkness as we walked there. "We can't stay too long," we told him. From what we knew about both the Miskitos and Brother Mike, we wouldn't have been completely shocked to see a roomful of naked people, a big barrel of mishlaw punch in the center, mattresses on all sides, and someone handing out free contraceptives at the door.

People still had their clothes on when we got there. There were children present, and old people. People leaning in the unscreened windows and packing into every corner of the room until the place looked more like a Jackson Pollock than a van Gogh. There was no mishlaw that I could see, but a bottle of something was going around outside. I took a hit: It was *guaro*.

We followed Brother Mike inside and somebody found seats for us. There were two guitars, a mouth harp, a washtub bass, and a turtle-shell drum . . . and another bottle of *guaro,* passed by a man who looked more like a French Creole from New Orleans than a Miskito. Fred Haylock, his name was, from Cauquira . . . a village across the lagoon on the coast. And the *guaro* was also creeping up on the master of ceremonies: a tall, thin guy with dreds and the generic name of Rasta.

It took the dancers, though, to convince us there was going to be actual dancing and not just some kind of musical . . . *prelude.* There were ten: five males, five females. They lined up in a businesslike way. The number was under way without any prelude at all: One minute people were standing and sitting around, the next they were chanting, playing, and dancing:

Usus mairin (Buzzard)
Usus mairin (Buzzard)
Namwa laki (Drying your wings)
Namwa laki (Drying your wings)
Bipkam biara (Cow's intestines)
Bipkam biara (Cow's intestines)
Drubi piram (Pull and eat them)
Drubi piram (Pull and eat them)

The dancers flopped around like buzzards flying, buzzards drying their wings, buzzards hopping, buzzards fighting over dead meat. The quavering melody line was picked up and repeated over and over by everyone present and soon Brother Mike was on his feet, moving quite lightly in his baggy khakis and vestment through the complicated steps on into other numbers and on into the night until you had to wonder: *Who was ministering unto whom?* Whatever it was, though, it looked like the real thing. And while it wasn't exactly a shock (I knew the Episcopal Church had changed, after all) it definitely took us by surprise.

We asked Rasta if we could take some photographs. He said he didn't think there would be a problem, once the fee had been settled. But when we finally left, people still had all their clothes on.

W E HEADED out to Brother Mike's church bright and early the next morning. It was all alone in the middle of the flat, treeless savanna outside of town . . . a palm thatched roof (with quite a few gaps) and rough-cut board siding. But the Cross of St. George was bravely emblazoned on the sign in front and the church bell was ringing out over the vast emptiness. Behind the altar, Brother Michael had painted a variety of New Testament tableaux featuring Jesus and the disciples as Miskito Indians. We took our places in the pews, along with the rest of the congregation: four men, one woman, three children.

The chapel at St. Paul's School had been built on the English model, with pews facing each other along a grand center aisle. The boys were ranked according to class: the youngest closest to the aisle, the seniors in ornately carved wooden seats in the back. We all wore coats and ties except for the choir, which wore surplices and cassocks. The huge organ, played by organist Channing Lefebvre, set the tone. The headmaster, Rev. Matthew Madison Warren—tall, straight, bald, steel-rimmed, thin-lipped, and very scary—conducted the service. Every day a senior was called on to read the lesson from a huge Bible on a brass lectern in the transcept . . . I was never chosen, either because my voice was too squeaky or because I had never bothered to get confirmed; I didn't ask. Then everyone filed out two by two, littlest first, past the waiting parents, faculty kids, and wives in the far rear, and past the area set aside for tardy students . . . who would be awarded their demerits later in the day. One of the masters is now bishop of Washington. The older brother of a classmate is now bishop of Chicago. And the uncle of another classmate has been bishop of New York.

It had been serious, so serious that when Brother Mike appeared from a little closet beside the burlap-covered altar in his brown robe I started nervously and couldn't look at him. Maybe it was the baldness. And singing the old familiar hymns in Miskito wasn't as amusing as I'd thought it would be . . . I kept waiting for that certain slant of light to reveal him in all his glory with the guilty knowledge that I'd been praying for him to make a fool out of himself.

He gave the sermon in both Miskito and English for our benefit. The theme was Adam and Eve and the apple. He explained that the story was about everyone's personal struggle with the devil, not who said what to whom in some garden thousands of years ago. "For example," he said, "last night I was asleep in my house and a woman came knocking on the door. 'Brother Mike, I'm lonely. Open the door and let me in.' "

Brother Mike grinned to see us leaning forward in our pew. "I knew my Bible," he said. "I knew what Jesus had done in the desert. I quoted the scriptures to her as Jesus did to the devil, and she disappeared."

Susan and I couldn't help but exchange glances.

"I challenge you all to study your Bible," Brother Mike said. Did he wink at us? Anyway, the ice was broken. And the rest of the congregation was smiling, too.

T HE CONGREGATION was all from Nicaragua: Episcopal missionaries had been busy there over the years. But the miserable record of missionaries in other parts of the world didn't hold true for the Miskitos ... the missionaries were accommodated like everyone else. The missionaries might not have saved a whole lot of souls ... Miskitos being what they are ... but they provided the health and education services that no government ever did.

We held our breath as Brother Michael whipped off his robe after the service but ... *i qué milagro!* ... underneath it were his serviceable khaki pants and a green hospital scrub vest. "Well, onward and upward." He had his four other churches to give services at, and quite a few vehicles to get to them in: a Jeep, a motorcycle, and an outboard-motor-powered cayuco. And it was kind of endearing, too, that none of the vehicles worked very well.

Brother Mike kept the faith. We left him tinkering with the Jeep and walked back into town. I found myself imagining him as headmaster of St. Paul's School and liking the idea a lot.

LINES WRITTEN BY A YOUNG ENGLISHMAN OF HIGH MORALS ON A HOT SUNDAY AFTERNOON IN MOS-QUITIA

The palm frond pushes senselessly against the wind,
Its leaves plastered back on the grey pate of sky.
In their shadow,
Brown, round-hipped girls

Take the burden of their mothers'
docile babes
Against their virgin flesh.

They await their own moment:
A hot sweat
And the jerk and cuff of limbs
In the tense silence of a lonely place,
Looking up into an unknown face.

Lost in the shock of being wanted
And opening up to smooth-gloved lust
Then marked
By the drip of bloody tears
That punctuate the years.

Fecundity seeps from the rich clay-colored
folds of their skin,
The abundance of mile-wide thighs
And blind, blind eyes to sin.

In the silver of a full moon
They follow a path of packed earth
That their mothers once trod
And bend
To the breath of man

—*Paul Stephenson, MOPAWI volunteer*

O N THE second-floor veranda of the house behind The Bunker we noticed a man lying on his stomach on a piece of foam rubber covered by a sheet. It looked cool and pleasant: The trade winds off the lagoon ruffled his hair and flapped the sheet . . . a nice way to nurse a hangover through a hot Sunday afternoon.

"*Es un buzo,*" someone told us when we nodded at him enviously. "*No puede movar.*" He's a diver . . . he can't move.

No, he wouldn't mind talking to us. We climbed the stairs into the heavy sweet smell of bedsore disinfectant and introduced ourselves. His bare upper body was smooth and slim as a young boy's and his handshake was warm and limp. His face was gray and triangular and he raised his head with difficulty to talk to us. He was completely paralyzed from the shoulders down.

His mother came out of her room and his older brother wandered across the yard to hear how the gringos were going to help. We told them we were only writers.

At about two A.M. in August 1989, the dive boat *Randy,* out of Grand Cayman, dropped anchor half a mile off the beach and began signaling with its spotlight. Half an hour later four *cayucos,* each carrying two men, appeared out of the blackness and were taken on board. The men went to sleep in their *cayucos* on the deck, stacked beside ten others already in place. In the morning, the *Randy* was butting through clean blue ocean swells on the way to Quita Sueño Bank for fifteen days of lobster diving. Keep-awake Bank, 120 miles east-southeast of Gracias a Dios, a coral reef rising from hundreds of fathoms of open ocean, marked by huge wrecked freighters and a couple of tiny cays where pirates had been marooned in the old days. There were human bones under some of the ledges.

The *Randy* was sixty feet long . . . almost all the space was hold. There were cabins for the captain, cook, and two deckhands. The ten Miskito divers and their ten *cayuqueros* (boatmen) slept in their *cayucos.* If they were lucky, they'd come back with 4,000 pounds of lobster tails in the hold, meaning as much as $25,000 gross and $300 to $500 for each dive team, depending on how many pounds they'd tallied.

The *Randy* was a straight boat, like most Grand Cayman vessels and unlike those from Guanaja, in the Bay Islands, whose captains always had a store of dope in the hold and whose divers wouldn't come if they didn't. Divers went aboard the *Randy* because they knew the captain wasn't going to make them work in bad weather and was going to keep the *salidas* to three a day. A diver dove three tanks on each *salida;* at the depths the lobster were to be found these days (sometimes 150 feet) nine tanks a day seemed plenty. No one on board wanted to do fifteen, and that too was a reason they were on this boat and not one from Guanaja. But no one on board was familiar with the U.S. Navy Decompression Tables, which would indicate that after even nine tanks a day at those depths a diver shouldn't be alive. And of course, when it came to judging depths, things were a little imprecise because no one had depth gauges. No one had watches or air pressure gauges either; they just started up when the airflow began to feel "heavy."

But the *Randy* was a perfect boat for Archimes, who was slender, serious, and a trifle effeminate. No hero. Archimes would have been content to remain a *cayuquero* forever if it hadn't been for the *sacabuzo* at The Bunker.

The *sacabuzo* (diver-hunter) was on the prowl for warm bodies. He had advanced Archimes more than $500 on wages so Archimes could buy his mother a new refrigerator; and there were other things. The upshot of it was that now he owed the *sacabuzo* several thousand . . . and the debt was growing. The *sacabuzo* was not so nice anymore and quite easily convinced Archimes that he should move on to diving: The pay was twice as good and anyway Archimes was a natural, according to the *sacabuzo*. Archimes himself thought otherwise but who was he to argue?

Archimes had never thought of himself as a diver and nei- ther had anyone else. At twenty-eight he still lived with his mother . . . there was no girlfriend in sight, much less a wife. Archimes didn't particularly enjoy drinking and dancing at The Bunker with the dive crowd and the dive crowd tended to laugh at Archimes when they saw him around town and to call him a nerd. Archimes didn't particularly care.

His first trip as a diver on the *Randy* had gone all right. At least, he hadn't seen the mermaid. He had paid off some of his debt to the *sacabuzo,* and almost managed to convince himself that maybe the *sacabuzo* had been correct. But that didn't stop the other divers from laughing at him. *"The mermaid is going to love Archimes. She's going to think he's another mermaid."*

THE WATER he dove in was clear as air. Sometimes, when he first jumped over the side, he'd get dizzy. He'd have a feeling he was going to fall seventy feet to the bottom.

The lobsters lived in dark caves. Sometimes, but not too often, they worked their way into a cul-de-sac and you could grab them with your gloves. Most of the time you had to hook them quickly with the *gancho* or they would disappear into the depths of the reef. You stabbed them once in the body with the pointed end of the *gancho* and left them on the bottom to pick up later. It was a problem trying to remember where you had left them before your air ran out. The light was dim down there, and everything seemed much bigger than it really was. There were always shapes moving on the edge of your vision.

ALMOST ALL the other divers had seen the mermaid. Some couldn't move their legs for five days afterwards. Some said that their legs were still numb and didn't work very well anymore on land. But they all said that when they got back in the water where the mermaid lives their legs worked fine. She wanted them near her.

The other divers' hair was bleached blondish from the fierce sun. Most of them were muscley and macho and used to being looked up to by women and children . . . the equivalent of cowboys in the American West. Archimes was a square peg in a round hole, but that didn't particularly bother him as long as the money was good. What bothered him were the big shapes moving on the edge of his vision off the drop-off in over a hundred feet of water.

He knew that the mermaid was not real. But one night he asked what she looked like.

There was nothing but laughter. As usual.

JUST AS Archimes was the most junior diver, his *cayuquero* was also the most junior: barely in his teens. There was no prestige in being a *cayuquero* for a nerd like Archimes; he'd been ordered to do it by his father, who wanted to get him started on a profitable life of diving as quickly as possible and knew that Archimes probably wouldn't be able to get anyone else. But aboard ship, the *cayuquero* avoided Archimes and behind his back made jokes about him to the others. *"He always says a prayer before he goes down, and do you know who it's to? His mother."* He was a good mimic. He imitated Archimes saying his prayers and crossing himself and everybody roared with laughter.

IN THE summer of 1989, the lobsters on Quita Sueño Bank were scarcer than anyone could remember. Seven days into the trip the hold was less than a quarter full and everyone was in a bad mood. They were looking for someone to pick on.

One of the divers had brought along a little *mota*. After the broiling sun roared down into the blue water, while the *Randy* rocked in the godforsaken anchorage and the laughter and talk of the white captain and crew floated on a cozy square of light from the wheelhouse where none of the divers was ever invited, he broke it out, rolled a joint and began passing it around. Soon everyone was feeling a lot better ... except for Archimes, who had never smoked *mota* and refused the joint. He shook his head at his young *cayuquero* when the joint got to him, but the boy just grinned, took an enormous drag and passed it on.

"Your mother would be very sad," Archimes said to the boy. Then he walked out to the *cayucos* to lie down.

"It would be funny to play a trick on him, don't you think?" the boy said to the others. He pointed at the gasoline compressor that was pumping up the tanks for the next day. "Look. Suppose I were to blow a little *mota* into the air intake of one of the tanks. It might make him feel more relaxed tomorrow ... poor man. He needs it."

The boy glowed in the laughter of his elders. He blew a few good lungfuls of smoke into the air intake and scratched a little cross onto the tank with a nail. It was all in fun, and most probably harmless.

T HE NEXT day was flat calm. Before the *Randy* left the anchorage, the captain called the divers together and announced a fifty-dollar reward to the man who got the day's largest catch. He said they'd be diving off the unprotected southern end of the bank where the drop-off was steepest and there were usually the most lobsters, when it was calm enough to dive. The young *cayuquero* thought he felt Archimes looking at him, but he didn't look back. He'd arranged to have the marked tank handed down, along with two others, for the first *salida*.

Archimes and the boy paddled the little *cayuco* over the bottomless indigo water toward the drop-off, visible 100 or so feet down by a shift from indigo to slightly lighter blue. It was only an hour after dawn, still cool and glassy. There were no sharks visible. The boy gleefully watched Archimes go through his prayer ritual; he put the marked tank into Archimes' dive vest, attached the regulator, and took a puff to see if it was working properly. The dope could not be smelled.

Archimes never talked before a dive. He put on the vest, spat in his mask and rinsed it, put on his flippers and gloves, and got ready to roll over the side with his *gancho* in his left hand. "Good luck, uncle," the boy said, with laughter rising in the back of his throat. The water was so clear he could see quite clearly the little dot that Archimes became at one hundred feet.

THERE WERE ten lobsters on Archimes' *gancho* when he surfaced half an hour later. His eyes were shining in a way that the boy had never seen before. "A cave," he said. "It's full ... hundreds. Hundreds and hundreds." The lobster tails looked about a pound apiece: ten pounds of tail for the first dive when twenty for the whole day is good.

Archimes took off the vest and stayed in the water beside the *cayuco* while the boy rigged a new tank. He kept his mask on and marked his place on the bottom every few seconds. "Quick, boy. We're drifting."

"How does it feel, uncle?"

"How does what feel?"

The boy shrugged and grinned. The lobsters were shamefully big and real.

"We could get fifty pounds here. It feels like that. Mark the place for the next *salida*."

"How do I do that, uncle?"

Archimes was gone.

By the end of the third tank there were twenty tails in the

bottom of the *cayuco*. The *Randy* was floating out in open water and a breeze was starting to come up.

"There's hundreds more. Hundreds. Did you mark the place?"

"I didn't know how, uncle."

"You sight it on something, *tonto*. A *cayuquero* has to know that."

"This is my first trip, uncle."

Archimes thought for a while. "Look. We can't take a chance. Here's what we'll do. I'll stay here in the water. You go back to the ship for the tanks. Hurry."

The boy looked at Archimes in the water, his shining eyes, and suddenly got very worried.

"I don't want to leave you here, uncle."

"I'll be all right, *tonto*. I feel lucky. Maybe the mermaid's on my side today."

The boy was shocked. "You didn't see her?"

"Who knows? Now, quick . . ."

T HE CAPTAIN knew exactly what had happened. "He's found a lobster hole, hasn't he? Holy Mother, twenty tails already." The boy handed the tails up, three more tanks were handed down. "Get back to him quick."

"Captain, let me tell you. I don't think he's thinking very well now. Shouldn't he rest between *salidas*?"

"What do you mean, not thinking well?"

The boy shrugged. "I . . ."

"He'll be all right. It's only his second *salida*, no? I've known divers who make five. Get back to him with those tanks or he'll never forgive you."

AFTER THE first tank, there were five more lobsters on the *gancho* but Archimes' hands were shaking with cold. "I felt a chill down there," he said. "I came up as fast as I could. I need to get in and warm up."

He rolled into the bottom of the *cayuco*. His face was gray. "Maybe I saw something."

"What was it, uncle?"

"Nothing. There are hundreds left." Then he said: "I can't feel my toes."

A HONDURAN POLICE boat took Archimes to Grand Cayman, where there was a hyperbaric chamber. He was there for three months. The captain of the *Randy* paid for the treatment, but the trip from Quita Sueño had taken fourteen hours and it was too late.

The other divers told the boy it hadn't been his fault at all, that Archimes should never have seen the mermaid on only four tanks. But then, as they knew, Archimes was not strong. It hadn't been the boy's fault . . . three puffs of dope: It was a joke, nothing more. But the boy left Lempira to live with his aunt in Tegucigalpa. He told his father he never wanted to see the ocean again.

IN 1987, the last year for which figures were available, Honduras exported $19 million of lobster tails, mostly to the United States. One of the first measures taken by Honduras's conservative, U.S.-educated new president, Rafael Callejas, was to lift the seasonal ban on lobster-diving indefinitely.

There are about 100 dive boats and some 1,500 divers in Honduras. You can tell the divers by their bleached hair, and, in some cases, the fact that they can't walk too well.

MOST OF our information came from Mimi Dagen, a Mennonite missionary who came to Puerto Lempira seven years ago with her husband Wilmer to start MOPAWI. She has been gathering the first figures and background on diving casualties ever compiled for Mosquitia:

- Since tank diving started in the early 1970s, there have been 120 divers paralyzed, 48 killed. Twenty-eight percent of the paralysis cases occurred in the last two years, as divers have had to go deeper and deeper (sometimes to 150 feet) to find lobsters.
- The divers affected were seventeen to forty-nine years old and had diving experience ranging from two months to eighteen years. Thirty affected divers had more than five years experience.
- Eighty percent of one sample of paralysis cases occurred in more than ninety feet of water.
- Only one case received hyperbaric-chamber treatment. The rest were treated with remedies varying from rum laced with garlic to injections of calcium.

Mimi Dagen, who has been the Honduran government's chief health officer for the province of Gracias a Dios, is applying for a grant from the World Rehabilitation Fund to pay for teachers and equipment. The teachers, who would be former divers, would circulate through the coastal villages of Mosquitia giving classes on basic diving techniques. And they would distribute the first underwater watches and depth gauges ever seen in these parts.

She and a Miskito ex-high school teacher and diver named Walstead Müller Aude have already started one divers' group in Puerto Lempira: *Pío Buzo*. They hope to organize similar groups in two other areas of diver concentration.

"The rumor is already out," she told us with an unmissionarylike grin. "MOPAWI is raising hell."

Four

Nicaragua

MYSELF have always felt quite strongly like an emerging country in Central America; most strongly like La Mosquitia, in fact: trying (but never quite succeeding) to come to terms with my seedy yet respectable ... *British* ... colonial past; my shadowy, inscrutable, rich, powerful ... *American* ... connections. I have crippling problems in dealing with outside authority, and yet I can never seem to get my own act together.

My father bombed at Eton, the hoary British "public school" that is certainly matrix of everything stiff-upper-lip and old-school-tie. And yet, a generation later in the Land of the Free, he beat the bushes to find St. Paul's ... the closest American equivalent ... so I could "succeed" where he had "failed." What we need (La Mosquitia and I) is definitely not more of the same.

I was sailing back into my own self.

NICARAGUA ... especially the Mosquito Coast of Nicaragua ... is the distillation of Central America, after all. It's the place where all the old issues are most clearly drawn ... a place of dust, battle, blood, death. A place where, out of necessity, you're supposed to find out who you are and who everyone else is, too. Which romantic notion is, of course, the reason I went to Vietnam as a reporter in the sixties.

The English literati W. H. Auden and Christopher Isherwood went to the Chinese front in 1938 in something of the same spirit. The book was called *Journey to a War*. They found themselves on a rickety Chinese train in the middle of the night waiting for the Japanese bombs:

> And there, right opposite, blazing from the blackness of the opposite shore like the illuminations of a pretentious roadhouse, were the Japanese searchlights. We yelled at them and waved our arms, suddenly hysterical as a drunken charabane party: "Come on! Shoot! Shoot!" ... Soon after, the guard came to tell us that we might relight our candles. We were safe. The train slackened speed a little. The passengers began to get ready for bed. "You see," said Auden. "I told you so ... I knew they wouldn't ... Nothing of that sort ever happens to *me*." "But it does to *me*," I objected; "and if it had this time you'd have been there, too." "Ah, but it didn't, you see." "No, but it might." "But it didn't."
> There is no arguing with the complacency of a mystic. I turned over and went to sleep.

I'd been only half joking when I'd repeated that line to Susan's worried daughters before we left. *Nothing of that sort ever happens to me.* It was, in fact, mostly true: I seemed to have been through one war, several near misses on the road, miscellaneous narrow squeaks and close shaves without so much as a scribble on the envelope of my mortality. Susan's daughters just looked at me with resentment—they had a strong feeling that things of that sort did happen to their mother—but I wasn't being complacent. And I don't think Auden was, either.

Things of that sort might happen to Susan, but she wanted to go anyway. Very much. Sometimes, in fact, she seemed more enthusiastic about the trip than I did; she made me feel jaded.

Either she welcomed the chance of things happening, or she felt safe with me: I never quite got around to asking.

WE DEVELOPED a strategy to use with pirates, if we saw any. They were reported to be operating south of Gracias a Dios out of small, seagoing *cayucos* equipped with outboards and probably not carrying more than five or six men. We had on board a Browning semiautomatic shotgun with a five-shot magazine.

The shotgun was chambered for three-inch shells . . . you can bring down a Canada goose with it at a range of almost a hundred yards. Goose shot-size is number 2 or 4. We had triple-ought buckshot shells that are mainly used by riot police or big-game hunters.

Our strategy was as follows: I'd stay hidden below while the pirates approached. Susan would engage them in conversation. If they seemed threatening or tried to get on board she'd drop to the floor of the cockpit and I'd blow them away through a porthole. Then, you might say rather cynically, we'd find out who we were all right.

If we'd thought there was any more than an outside chance of this happening, we would have taken the offshore route. You have to believe me. But, as they say on Wall Street: no risk, no reward. The reward was being the first American boat since the revolution to *peacefully* sail the northern Caribbean coast of Nicaragua.

WE ANCHORED inside the shallow (five-foot) bar at the mouth of the inlet to Caratasca Lagoon on the evening of March 9, thinking to leave the next morning and be in Puerto

Viejo, the Nicaraguan harbor just south of Cabo Gracias a Dios, well before sundown. It was less than fifty miles: a day's trip. And we'd be well inside the limit of our precious Nicaraguan visa, which had to be used by March 13.

Boat life being what it is, we limped into Puerto Viejo March 18. The visa had expired, but that was the least of our worries . . . in the good old tradition of the place, we were giving *Gracias a Dios* that we had gotten there at all.

March 10: *Up at 5:15 A.M. but too rough to leave. Bar is breaking heavily all across. In the afternoon a freighter tries to come in but grounds on the sand. Waves break over ship . . . he finally backs off and anchors in deeper water to wait. Two other ships out there waiting.*

March 11: *Still too rough to leave . . .*

March 12: *Leave at six A.M., with rudder strut smashing sickenly on bottom. Dead beat to Gracias against a twenty-five-knot wind so decide to tack out to Vivorillo Cays thirty miles northeast, spend night, and tack back the next day to Gracias. Find cays okay in spite of SATNAV malfunction . . . very remote, lonely, beautiful, scary.*

March 13: *Too windy to risk Gracias. Work all day fruitlessly on autopilot . . . it only turns the boat to starboard. Also, winch clutch burns out again. A horrible feeling that it is all too much, miles from anyplace and facing a very tricky leg.*

March 14: *Showers and howling wind all night . . . by morning has shifted southeast! Now a dead beat to Gracias from here and still too windy anyway. Second day working fruitlessly on autopilot. Also, now the outboard motor doesn't work either.*

March 15: *Jury-rig autopilot but sacrifice my own body. Same symptoms as autopilot . . . my brain sends signals to my left foot, but the foot doesn't work, just flops helplessly. Crouching in engine room for two days has deadened the nerve. Susan fixes winch and outboard with my direction . . . now the ship is 100 percent, but the old bod is seriously disabled.*

March 16: Ceaseless twenty-knot southeast trade (that hasn't let up for two weeks now) and news from Dr. Welch on the radio that I have to lie in bed for at least two days without moving.

March 17: First reasonably calm day in two weeks. Wind shifts back to east. Why? Because there is a cold front on the way, according to Coast Guard weather in Portsmouth, Virginia. So we have to leave at sunset, even though my foot doesn't work.

March 18: Terrible night. Autopilot repairs only last for two hours, and alternator/waterpump belt breaks: We have to spend three hours fixing it at night, in a godforsaken lumpy sea, with bad backs and a numb foot . . .

O F COURSE we weren't the only ones to have trouble in these parts:

I reached Cape Gracias a Dios and from there on Our Lord gave me favoring wind and current. This was on 12 September. For 88 days (*sic*) the terrifying hurricane had pursued me, so that I saw neither the sun nor the stars because of the sea. The seams of the vessels spread, the sails were split, anchors, rigging, cables, boats and many of the stores lost; the people exhausted and so down in the mouth that they were all the time making vows to be good, to go on pilgramages and all that; yea, even hearing one another's confessions! Other tempests have I seen, but none that lasted so long or as grim as this. Many old hands whom we looked on as stout fellows lost their courage. What griped me most were the sufferings of my son; to think that so young a lad, only thirteen, should undergo so much . . . I was sick and many times lay at death's door . . . My brother was in the worst of the vessels, the most dangerous, and I felt terribly, having persuaded him to ship against his will . . . (From Columbus's *Lettera Rarissima* to the Sovereigns, 7 July 1503)

I'm not trying to impress Queen Isabella; I'm not going to make a big plea for sympathy. What we went through wasn't that bad. It just wasn't. But sufficient unto the day is the evil thereof. When we finally sighted Cabo Gracias a Dios, low and gray in the hazy early morning sun, we cheered and had another cup of coffee and offered up our meager thanks.

T HERE WAS no sign of life at the cape itself, where the Río Coco, the Wankie, the Wanks, the Cape, or the Segovia (depending on your politics) empties into the Caribbean. The navigation light wasn't working; the radio towers that the Coast Pilot said we'd be able to see were not visible, or were nonexistent. There was no little town at the mouth of the river, such as appears on some charts. The sea was brown and lumpy, as usual. The sun had disappeared behind undifferentiated gray cirrus.

Frankly it looked like the end of the world. But, to look on the bright side, there were no pirates . . . a far cry from the way it used to be in the good old seventeenth century when Gracias a Dios was the buccaneers' harbor of choice.

We sailed in under the cape, into Nicaraguan waters. At the base of the cape we could see the mouth of a lagoon, breaking all across in the chop: much too shallow for entry. On the far side of the lagoon we could see some houses. There was no protection from the east wind anywhere so when the depth shallowed to eight feet or so in front of the bar we dropped anchor.

We were pitching in the chop, but at least we weren't rolling. It was midmorning. We fell into our bunk, but soon the *Lord Jim* was surrounded by cayucos filled with curious men. Some of them thought we were a dive boat come to pick up lobster divers. Some thought we were a relief ship with supplies from the United States.

"We're tourists," I said in Spanish. "We have sailed all the way from the United States. We need to get some sleep. We'll come in later."

"They are tourists," the man in the lead cayuco explained to the others in Spanish. "They have sailed all the way from the United States. They need to get some sleep. They'll come in later." He turned back to us and suddenly smiled. "Welcome to Nicaragua."

IN COLUMBUS'S day and for two hundred years afterward, Puerto Viejo had been a wonderful anchorage. The lagoon had been deep, the entrance easily passable. By the mid-eighteenth century the buccaneers had been translated into "respectable" British settlers; they and their slaves had established large sugar plantations along the Río Coco and Puerto Viejo harbor was full of trading ships.

Puerto Viejo was also, not coincidentally, the residence of the Mosquito Kings. The name of the inspired Brit who first came up with the idea of starting the monarchy is lost to history . . . but no matter: No one cracked a smile and the "coronations" in Belize and Jamaica gradually took on a legitimacy directly in proportion to the pomp and circumstance:

> After cards of invitation were sent to the merchants . . . the dignitaries and townspeople gathered for a parade on the appointed morning, then set out for the church. George Frederick (the Mosquito King), in the uniform of a British major, rode horseback between two attendant British officers and his chiefs followed in double file, dressed in sailors' trousers. At the church, the coronation service was read by the chaplain of the Belize colony in the name of the Archbishop of Canterbury,

amid the roar of cannon salutes by vessels in the harbor. The regalia were a silver gilt crown, a sword, and a scepter of small value. The chiefs were not allowed to swear their allegiance to the new king until they were baptized (during the same ceremony). After retiring to a school-room for the coronation dinner, the new king and his subjects became intoxicated, then fell asleep on the floor. After this revelry was over, the British authorities put the king and his retinue aboard a British vessel, that took them back to Cape Gracias a Dios. (Peter F. Stout, *Nicaragua: Past, Present and Future,* Philadelphia, 1859)

The British-educated Mosquito Kings developed a love for the perquisites of royalty themselves—slaves, nice clothes, firearms, good wine and whiskey—and sometimes they were a little difficult to control. But they and the British understood each other in ways that sometimes must have been embarrassing to both of them and if it hadn't been for forces outside either's control the system might well still be in existence. It was a lot like being sent to St. Paul's School, so to me the whole familiar idea was both hateful and fascinating.

External forces wrecked Puerto Viejo, too. In the mid-eighteenth century the British dug a canal from the Río Coco to the lagoon for the easy transportation of sugar to the trading ships. Within ten years or so the river had silted up the harbor and made it useless. And by the early nineteenth century, Puerto Viejo was much like it is now:

Only a few houses; and those, with the exception of the King's, that of Dalby, one of his chiefs, and an old merchant's of the name of Bogg, of the very worst description, being mere huts, barely sufficient to protect the natives from the weather. (From Roberts, *Voyages and Excursions in Central America,* 1827)

Midafternoon. We poled the inflatable over the shallow bar into the lagoon and motored slowly across to the houses, running aground every few minutes. Many of the trees onshore looked dead and the predominant landscape color was gray. But mullet were jumping and a flock of teal took off and circled away over the dead trees. There were blue crabs dancing over the muddy sand bottom, and whelks. We anchored the boat in six inches about a quarter of a mile from shore and waded in, the water hot around our ankles. Some kids playing in the shallows stopped playing and watched us with enormous eyes.

There were soldiers on the shore watching us, too. They carried AK-47s, grenades, bandoliers, light machine guns, knives, and pistols, and were dressed in tight-fitting tiger-stripe fatigues. We did our best to ignore them and headed for a small group of civilians who seemed to be having a conversation in the shallows. They looked earnest, but friendly; we told them we had come to pay our respects to Señor Coronado López. The name worked magic, and behind it lies a story . . .

From the beginning of our time in La Mosquitia, I had had an unexplained fascination for a renegade Miskito leader with the wonderful name of Steadman Fagoth. He had been jailed by Somoza as a "communist" and by the Sandinistas as a Somozan / CIA agent and "separatist" . . . and in 1985, was expelled from Honduras after threatening at a press conference to execute twenty-three Nicaraguan soldiers captured by his Honduran-based guerrillas. He had clearly been too much to handle, even for the CIA.

One of the Contras we talked to in Honduras said Fagoth was "loco . . . just eating green mangoes." Another said he was "just out for himself . . . a loose cannon." But the fact was, he had almost single-handedly organized the Miskito refugees in Honduras into effective guerrillas and had led them for three years until people got tired of his strong-arming. And we were to come across his strange little book, with no publisher or publication date listed, featuring a picture of Fagoth in fatigues, a beret, full beard, long hair—a dead ringer for Che—calling for an "autonomous region" for the Miskito people.

Father John Samsa, the Catholic priest we talked to in Puerto Lempira, told us he had heard that Fagoth was now officially back in Nicaragua working with the Sandinistas on repatriation of refugees. We also heard he had a wife and children who lived in Honduras in a little village just across the lagoon from Puerto Lempira. And that he visited them often.

He was violent (some said brutal), unpredictable, power-hungry, and possibly opportunistic ... but I felt some kind of bond with him, God help me. So before we left Honduras we had gone to the little village (Cauquira) to look for him.

S TEADMAN'S WIFE Ora was away somewhere with the children, but we met his father-in-law Duval Haylock, who owned a big dive boat, lived in a fancy house on a point of land across a waterway from the one-street town and was definitely a village elder. He invited us over to meet his other daughter, Clara.

Clara was thirty-eight and still shockingly beautiful, even though she was putting on a little weight and middle age was loitering around the corner. A red hibiscus in her black hair; a dark blue silk South Sea Island dress with yellow floral designs against her smoky skin; the white seashell smile and the invitation of a sideways tilt of her head: Fifteen years earlier she was the girl in the postcard you sent home from Tahiti: *And this is paradise; wish you were here ...*

She carried herself like royalty, like she knew her father wanted her to ... *a Miskito princess* ... but you could see she was not quite happy.

Duval Haylock had sent her to America at the earliest possible opportunity: at seventeen, with the Experiment in International Living. To (where else?) Los Angeles. This was her first time home in almost fifteen years. Her ex-husband (they met at the University of California at Irvine) still lives in Orange County. Their son, a very gringo-looking kid of two, lives with her. She had separated from her husband in the last year.

We asked her if she planned to stay in Cauquira . . . *here in paradise.*

"Oh no," she said not quite happily but in perfect California English. "I'll be going back to Orange County." She watched her son rolling a model airplane through the sand. "For him, you know. The schools." She took off her shoes and almost threw them on the ground. "I'll show you around, if you want."

W E TOOK off our own shoes and followed her along the sandy paths. On the other side of a grove of palms, on pilings over the waterway, a new house was going up: Steadman and Ora's. The roof was already on and a few family things were inside. Clara picked up a photo album and we saw that her sister Ora was not as amazingly beautiful, but probably more bouncy. She and Steadman and their two kids were lying cozily together on a big bed looking very domestic; we could see that the hair on top of Steadman's head was thinning, making him look less like Che Guevara and more like a perennial graduate student.

They had met on this same ground when Steadman—whose mother was Ora's grandfather's niece—came to visit from his hometown, Bilwaskarma on the Río Coco, which forms the Honduran-Nicaraguan border. At the time he was about ten or twelve; they met again as college students in Costa Rica. They had the two children, but never got around to marrying.

Farther along the sandy path, in the middle of the neck of land, was the bungalow of Clara and Ora's grandfather Müller, Steadman's great-uncle, of German parentage by way of Texas. Nobody was quite sure how old he was, but he looked about ninety to us . . . although very spry in high rise pants and bright red fireman's suspenders. Müller: A lot of people have that name in Mosquitia . . . we were too delicate to ask exactly how they came by it.

Back at her father's house, Clara presented us with a copy of Steadman Fagoth's curious book—rumored to have been published in Miami with the help of the CIA—claiming that the Sandinistas had "disappeared" more than 250 Miskitos in 1981 and eighty-two alone and destroyed eighty-one towns in the Río Coco area:

> Our fundamental right to autodetermination is an "aboriginal right." The indigenous population has had this right from the beginning and it has been the dominant immigrant population which has violated this right, above all where the indigenous population were not in a condition to resist. Because of this, in the light of historic truth, we are able to maintain that the systems of social production of the country are not progressive ones but rather a consequence of external colonial forces, which have trampled our indigenous nations, almost completely exterminating them in the Pacific region, and are living on in the Atlantic region of the country, where the indigenous population today raises its fundamental claim: RECOGNITION BY THE NICARAGUAN STATE OF ITS TERRITORY AND REGIONAL AUTONOMY. (Translated from the Spanish)

"Steadman is due to visit any day now," she said. "You could wait."

"How does he come?"

"He comes in through the army base. They handle his transportation."

"Where is he now?"

She shrugged and smiled. "He moves around a lot."

"You must be very proud of him."

"Of course we are."

But we had only two days left to use our Nicaraguan visa and we couldn't stay. "Maybe we'll see you in Los Angeles," I said.

"Yes, maybe."

She stood in the warm ankle-deep water of her childhood (in a strange way, my own childhood), looking not quite happy, and watched us go. When we waved, she lifted her hand to the height of her shoulder for a minute and then let it drop. We looked back just before we rounded a bend in the waterway; she was still standing there.

D UVAL HAYLOCK had told us to look up his friend Coronado López when we got to Puerto Viejo; that's how we got the name . . . a name to conjure with, as it turned out. Now we found ourselves talking (in Spanish) to the wiry, dark, intense Moravian lay pastor (*sasmalkra*) of the village, who smiled a reassuringly twenty-four-carat smile and indicated the lounging soldiers: "These are our *Yatama* boys. You're familiar with them?"

"Of course." We did our best to look as if we were very familiar with them. And they smiled and nodded back. *Yatama* was the current name for the Miskito guerrilla organization, formerly led by Steadman Fagoth. But that didn't entirely explain what they were doing in this village, which we'd thought was still under Sandinista control.

"It's Sunday, you know," the pastor said. "They are just visiting. Relaxing." And we could indeed see that along with the armament some of them had gloves, bats, and balls. We still weren't sure what they were doing here but we let it go. We had a camera and would have loved to have taken some pictures, but we let that go, too.

The pastor said that Coronado López lived more than a mile away at the other end of town, but that he would be happy to take us there. We set off, along with half the village, and the soldiers went back to playing baseball. It looked pretty dangerous, with all those grenades.

With my left foot flopping down so that every once in a while I'd catch my toes on the ground, we paraded between two lines of huts on stilts along the footpath which was the town's only road. Groups of kids ran up, men stopped talking and waved, women came to the doors of their houses and watched. We were being received like the French had received the GIs in the liberation of Paris . . . you'd have to call it embarrassing.

The pastor, whose name was Richard Benjamin, introduced us to everybody we passed and between introductions kept up a running commentary on what had happened to the town since the revolution. He showed us the ruins of the church, the school, a few stores, the meetinghouse. "All burned . . . they destroyed everything in 1982, cut down the palm trees, the mangoes, uprooted the crops, shot the cattle."

"What happened to the people?"

"Everybody left. Most of them went to Honduras, to the camps. They started to come back in 1985, but there are still many people in the camps."

We noticed that the people in town were either young, in their twenties, or in their fifties or older. All the young men had a strange pantherlike look. "Yes," Richard Benjamin said significantly, "there are many young men in the village now."

In the center of town, a blue-and-gray flag was flying from the flagpole. The *Yatama* flag, Richard Benjamin explained. "Of course."

"And the Sandinistas?"

"The last raid they made here was seven months ago."

There were no stores, no schools, no electricity, no roads. There was only one passenger/freight boat, a twenty-foot sailboat, that made trips sixty miles south to Puerto Cabezas when necessary. Otherwise you had to walk along the beach. Most people bought their supplies in Honduras; they were about two-thirds cheaper and the selection was three times as good. Crossing the border seemed no problem at all.

Asking how Puerto Viejans made a living wasn't that easy, but the answer was simple: They lived off the land and sold alligator skins. Sometimes they might catch one of the huge green sea turtles that used to be the Miskitos' buffalo. But green turtles these days were few and far between.

"And here is our church," said Richard Benjamin, pointing at a bare piece of ground covered with a tin roof on four poles.

C ORONADO LÓPEZ lived out on a point at the end of the road, in a kind of family compound which included the López cemetery and about four houses of relatives. He was white-haired, sixtyish, and very ill, according to Richard Benjamin, but supported himself with a slightly terrifying fragile dignity. We wanted to ask Coronado López if he was descended from the Mosquito Kings, but things being what they were, we let that go. Right then, instead of a crown, he was wearing a jaguar-skin hat.

A large crowd of the López family added itself to the crowd that was already around us. "We come from Cauquira," I said. "Duval Haylock sends you *saludos,* and hopes that everything is well here."

Coronado López inclined his head regally. His wife embraced Susan and said "Thank God you've come."

We couldn't think of much else to say, but it didn't matter. The occasion was already set: The United States, through its emissaries, was paying its respects to the chief (the king?) of the newly liberated village of Puerto Viejo. *Saludos y bienvenidos, amigos.* We come in peace and goodwill . . .

It was not the role I would have picked out for myself, but

everybody was having a terrific time and nobody gave it a second thought. A cassette player flipped on and suddenly we were listening to Bruce Springsteen's "Born in the USA." I swear to God.

THE LIGHT was beginning to fade, and we needed it to navigate our way back out of the lagoon. We began to take our leave of Coronado López, but he asked his wife to bring him his canes and set out with us, along with the rest of his family. The procession had grown to about fifty people.

Richard Benjamin respectfully fell back in the line so we were walking alone with Coronado López. He was having a harder time than I was. Moving his two canes slowly and deliberately ahead of his two feet, he began to tell us about *Los Días de Somoza:* quite literally The Good Old Days.

In the Good Old Days, there was an airstrip.

In the Good Old Days, there was a fish processing plant.

In the Good Old Days, bananas were lightered out to banana boats which took them to Puerto Cabezas and returned with supplies for the stores.

"You must be very happy at the way things have turned out," I said.

"We'll see." He was making a pronouncement. "We are waiting for *El Veintecinco* [April 25, when the Sandinistas were due to turn over the government to Violeta Chamorro]. Then we can be happy or not, depending."

I CAME VERY close to asking him then about the Mosquito Kings and all that, but I was distracted by Richard Benjamin; he was telling someone he had to go to Puerto Cabezas the next day but the twenty-foot sailing *cayuco* which was the only means of transportation wasn't leaving for a week.

It was perfect. "We have plenty of room," I said. "Why don't you come with us?" With the Moravian pastor in the boat, I figured, the pirates operating out of Sandy Bay about thirty miles south would be less likely to give us trouble.

"Muy bien," he said quickly. "But I have some friends with me."

"Bring them too."

He smiled his twenty-four-carat smile and nodded. Soon everybody was talking about the good life in Puerto Cabezas . . . a place where you could actually go into a bar and drink a few cold beers. There was festive gunfire behind us: A couple of Yatama soldiers were firing their AK-47s at a flock of wild parrots.

It was dark when we finally shook Coronado López' hand and headed back out to the inflatable; Richard Benjamin sent two teenagers with us in a *cayuco* to show us the channel.

"Are we going to be all right out there tonight?" we asked him.

"Claro. There are nothing but friends here."

"THAT WAS pretty strange, wasn't it?" I said to Susan in the cockpit of the *Lord Jim* after the two teenagers had disappeared into the night.

"What was?"

"That . . . *welcome.*"

"I thought it was wonderful." Her eyes were shining. "It was one of the most touching things I've ever been through. It made me proud to be an American."

I couldn't believe I'd heard properly. "What?"

"I said, it made me proud to be an American."

I shook my head. "You're *proud* of what we did to this country over the last 150 years?"

"I didn't say that."

"What did you say, then."

"I'm not talking about the last 150 years. I'm talking about what just happened in there."

"Well, so am I."

It seemed that Susan and I were on different sides, for the first time in the voyage. Nicaragua will do that.

THE ANCHORAGE was the worst we'd ever been in. There was zero protection from the east wind and the chop rose in the night to about four feet. It was as if we were anchored in the open ocean. I'd thought I was about ready for another significant dream, but it was too rough to dream; you just had to hang on. Also, I have to admit, I was worried about pirates. I went on deck every few hours to check for them: There was no light anywhere, either from the sky, the sea, or the land. It was all sound and movement. The warm wind zinged in the rigging, the boat leaped, creaked, and slatted, and the waves rolled by with a noise like rapids in a fast river.

AT DAWN two *cayucos* came out with Richard Benjamin and his friends: a serious young man named José and his chunky, quiet wife. José was one of Coronado López' legion of children.

It was about sixty miles to Puerto Cabezas ... Bragman's Bluff, as it was called in the old days of the British ... all easy protected sailing in the Miskito Channel between the coast and the cays. The CIA and the Contras had used the channel in the past for night speedboat raids on Puerto Cabezas, the main shipping port for northeast Nicaragua. Now the pirates used it. I planned to keep offshore as far as I could, on the outside edge of the channel, but we would still be visible from Sandy Bay. Our passengers didn't seem particularly worried.

The wind was on our beam, for the first time since we'd left Guatemala . . . a lifetime ago. The sky was nice and blue. And, as we got farther from shore, the water turned to aquamarine and began to sparkle. Cruising weather.

I passed out watery Honduran beer, and our passengers indulged their one moment of national chauvinism: Nicaraguan Victoria beer was much better.

"I have to ask you something," I said to José. "Is your father . . . are you . . . descended from the Mosquito Kings?"

"Es posible."

"Es probable." It was his wife Jean.

"The Mosquito Kings," I said. "That's . . . incredible." I wished my Spanish was better.

They nodded matter-of-factly.

I smiled. "Well, I should be honored that you are here on my boat." I meant it half-jokingly.

"The Miskitos need a king now," said Richard Benjamin very seriously. "God knows. They must have a leader."

I went below and got Steadman Fagoth's curious little book. "What about Steadman?"

Richard Benjamin's face lit up and he took the book into his hands as if he was taking the sacrament. His lips moved as he turned the pages. And I began to wonder very seriously if it would be a good idea for the Sandinistas in Cabezas to see him on board the *Lord Jim.*

"This is it," he told the others. "Listen to this." He began reading large sections of the book aloud in rapid Spanish. I remembered that Father John had told us that sometimes the pirates used a launch known to belong to the Moravian Church.

"Where is Steadman now?" I asked.

"He is in Puerto Cabezas. Working. For the Miskito people."

"Do you know him?"

"*Claro.*"

"Do you think you could arrange for us to meet him?"

"It is possible." Richard Benjamin thought for a while and laughed. "I tell you what. He'll probably be waiting for you on the pier. He always said he'd be there to welcome the first American boat when it came in."

W E MADE our approach to Puerto Cabezas on a blinding white Central American afternoon. Sheets of light flew from every moving surface of the chromium water; the land was a light gray haze between the water and the chromium sky. In all that storm of light the boat seemed invisible . . . no doubt the reason we hadn't been spotted by pirates.

We decided that the best strategy to explain the presence of Richard Benjamin and his friends was to say that we had been forced into Puerto Viejo by engine trouble. While we were fixing it, they had paddled out and asked for a lift. We had never gone ashore. Explaining the fact that our visa had expired was another matter.

"Maybe there won't be anybody around and you can just go ashore without notice," I said.

"There is always somebody around." Richard Benjamin looked pissed off and worried. He was not talking about Steadman. "The Sandinistas," he said. *"Enemigos de la humanidad."* I didn't find out until later that he was paraphrasing the Sandinista anthem: *Luchamos contra el yanqui, enemigo de la humanidad.* Let us fight the Yankee, the enemy of humanity.

It was a high earth bluff above a straight beach, with no

coves, no protection anywhere along it. There were some big stately buildings on the bluff that Richard Benjamin said were the convent and the convent school. Farther south a half-mile long wooden pier stuck out from the beach into the open ocean. The pier was built for freighters and shrimp boats and was about twenty feet above the water. The swells rolled right under it, but it did cut the wind a little. We dropped anchor a hundred feet or so to "leeward," behind some rusty Nicaraguan shrimp boats and a clean well-maintained one called the *Lady Lena,* from Roatán. Confiscated.

We felt very visible, with our American flag. Richard Benjamin assured us that "they" would be coming out immediately.

We waited for a half hour, but nobody came. "Things appear to have changed," Richard Benjamin said with great satisfaction. "They used to have a machine gun on the end of the pier. In the old days, if you came here at night, they'd shoot you."

I suggested calling on the VHF, but Richard Benjamin said that Sandinista frequencies were different "so no one could talk to foreign ships."

"Maybe we should go ashore and find them then," I said.

Richard Benjamin shrugged disdainfully. If there was nothing to fear from them anymore, why bother? And indeed, after we'd clambered (pretty floppily in my case) up onto the high pier, walked ashore, and found the little *Capitania del Puerto,* the *Capitania* seemed more scared of us than we were of him. But it was too late for the heavies, the Immigration people. We'd have to see them the next day.

A S THE sun went down, small groups of people strolled up and down the pier watching our insane pitching and rolling; maybe one of them was Steadman Fagoth . . . who Richard Benjamin promised we'd be meeting tomorrow.

But we were facing our third night of 80 percent sleeplessness. And it was suddenly, now that the excitement of arriving was over, enough to make strong people weep.

We heated a can of chili and ate it with the last of our watery Honduran beer. It was all we could manage. There were no lights on the pier when the sun had gone and almost no lights in the town. The waves crashed against the invisible pilings and there was absolutely no hope of getting ashore to the Seaman's Bar. We braced ourselves in separate bunks and tried to occupy our moments one by one.

S OMEBODY WAS hailing us from nearby. The moment of sunrise had followed all the other moments, as we had been pretty sure it would. It was a black guy in a white guayabera shirt, ferried out by one of the cayucos: He looked like some kind of official.

He hauled himself puppyishly on board. "My name's Cliff," he said in English. "Call sign Yankee November Seven Charlie Lima. You're hams, aren't you?" He was giving our radio equipment an eager once over: One of his boat-living American contacts had promised to show up in Puerto Cabezas and he'd been sure it was us.

When I told him I didn't have a license his face collapsed. "I'm very sorry," I said. "Please. Have a cup of coffee. It's Honduran." I don't know why I told him that.

Cliff was from Bluefields, Nicaragua's main port on the Caribbean 125 miles farther south. He was working here as an administrator for *Médicos sin Fronteras*—Doctors without Frontiers—a Dutch-run program that must have been related to the Guatemalan *Veterinarios sin Fronteras*, that I had had such a good experience with.

"Why don't you have a ham license?" he asked sadly.

"It's too hard to get in the United States. You have to know Morse code."

His face brightened. "So. Why don't you use a Nicaraguan call sign? I'll give you one right now. You are Yankee November Seven Golf Charlie."

"But . . ."

"No, it's nothing. We owe it to you."

The impromtu call sign has indeed been very useful . . . among other things enabling us to take advantage of the "Central American Breakfast Club," a net of mostly American ham boat people trading information up and down the coast. They were said to be sticklers for proper ham protocol—including legitimate U.S. licenses—but no one ever questioned us. God knows who they thought we were.

THE MOMENT of truth was at hand: our visit to the Immigration office. We dressed in our best clothes, got all our important papers together, and rowed over to the pier.

The shrimp boat that we'd used to climb out on before was gone; now it was a matter of monkeying our way straight up the pilings, with the inflatable rising and falling six feet in the swells. A huge crowd of loiterers (all men) gathered above us and Susan rose effortlessly, helped by a hundred hands.

"What about me?" I yelled. But everybody was occupied.

I put my floppy left foot in a loop of rope hanging from the piling and tried to lift myself. In a second, the brown water under the pier had closed over my head, my glasses were gone, and there were big splinters of wood under almost every fingernail. Susan said later that there was a "shocked silence" up on the pier. Fortunately she had the papers.

I rowed back out to the *Lord Jim,* doctored my hands, changed my clothes, and found my spare pair of glasses. I got some help the next time, but my fingers were numb and bleeding and so was my composure. It took two painful months for the splinters to grow out, my foot was flopping like a dying fish . . . meanwhile Susan was looking like a graduate of increasingly expensive Elizabeth Arden treatments. And I thought ruefully of W. H. Auden: *Nothing of that sort ever happens to me.*

I N THE end, it turned out to be a simple question of money . . . American dollars, to be precise: $25 U.S. for Immigration and $175 U.S. for Customs. Our elation seriously tempered by financial worries, we walked along red clay roads to the bank to change our traveler's checks.

Richard Benjamin had showed up to guide us around; he hadn't yet made contact with Steadman. The little town (pop. 12,000) reminded me of a Texas Panhandle town in summer—windswept, gritty, raw, blazing hot—but the walls featured wonderfully painted political murals. The Miskitos on the streets lacked the van Gogh colors of Honduran Miskitos but were faster moving: Vietnamese as compared to Cambodians. They paid no attention to us because, as Richard Benjamin explained, they thought we were Russian or Cuban. The pathetically understocked stores were run by Chinese and were full of people standing around drinking Victoria beer. I tried one: It *was* better.

Ortega campaign signs were everywhere, with their touching slogan: *todo será mejor.* Everything will be better. People were wearing Daniel T-shirts and hats and carrying Daniel bags: campaign souvenirs. There was nothing to indicate Chamorro even existed, although Richard Benjamin told us that she had won the district by at least 9 percentage points. "She came here in an old rented truck," he said. "And when she spoke, nobody could hear her because she had no sound equipment."

"I guess it didn't matter," I laughed.

"It made things better for her."

"But what about the polls?" I asked. "All the polls before the election said Ortega was going to win easily."

Richard Benjamin smiled disdainfully. "Do you think we would tell them what we were going to do?"

THE ONLY other client in the bank was a gringo . . . a Swiss construction expert. He shook his head at us on the way out. "Thin pickings."

The teller informed us that he couldn't give us dollars for our traveler's checks: New orders from Managua said that dollars were no longer available. He agreed to write us a note to that effect that we could give to Immigration and Customs; meanwhile he gave us 2.8 million córdobas for forty dollars in traveler's checks. The 100,000 córdoba bills were old 100 córdoba bills with the numerals inked over and changed. The ink came off on your hands.

We walked to the Immigration office and handed the note to the lieutenant. *"Qué clavo,"* he said: That just about nails it. He turned the note slowly over and over in his hands and finally said he would accept the traveler's checks. Anything but córdobas.

We walked to the Customs office. The chief (who looked East Indian, rather than Ladino like most Sandinista officials) said that he too would accept the traveler's checks but added that we would have to hire a shipping agent to prepare all the paperwork. And that would cost another $100 U.S.

WE PASSED the former convent, nicely situated on the edge of the bluff in a grove of big old pine trees and surrounded by the grassy playing fields of the convent school across the road. It was made from stucco in a Victorian style, with many turrets and extensions: by far the most imposing building in Puerto Cabezas.

"This is a place of evil," Richard Benjamin muttered.

"What do you mean?" We had noticed that many of the windows were barred but were prepared to write it off to Moravian-Catholic antipathy.

Richard Benjamin explained that after the revolution the convent had been turned into the local Sandinista headquarters. "Many people I know went in there, but only a few came out. There were tortures. And then the people were killed."

"How long did that go on?"

"Two cursed years after the revolution, 1981 and 1982, when they decided the Miskitos were their enemies. But it's not worth talking about because nothing I can tell you will make you know how bad it was."

He stood there looking at the ground while we watched the trade wind moving the dark pine trees against the stucco.

"What is the building used for now?" I asked after a while.

"It's the Ministry of Health office now." A ghostly little smile. "You see how healthy are all the people who are still alive?"

WE TOOK Richard Benjamin to lunch in the best restaurant in Puerto Cabezas, the Costa Brava: an attractive open-air place on the bluff overlooking the ocean. Jimmy Carter had eaten there during the election. A table of gringo-looking men were the only other diners. Richard Benjamin said they were Cubans.

"Prices have skyrocketed in the last two weeks," the owner told us sadly. "Nobody can afford to eat here now."

He stood beside the table, polite and hesitant, but with other things on his mind. "I have two children, señor. At least with the Sandinistas we had free schools. People are worried: What happens now? We had to pay under Somoza and now there is no money."

The lunch was delicious and cost 800,000 córdobas (about $11.50 U.S.). Richard Benjamin took some papers from his pocket: his wage stubs. As Moravian pastor of Puerto Viejo he made 600,000 córdobas per month; half of that was subtracted for board and medical insurance. A whole month's wages for him might have paid for dessert at the Costa Brava.

I told Susan I'd meet her down at the Seaman's Bar and went to the shipping agent.

O N THE way back to the Customs office with the shipping agent's *Vogue*-sized sheaf of forms, a black man in a white guayabera shirt hailed me: It was Cliff. He took me inside a building to meet a friend. Who should be sitting there too but the East Indian Customs chief?

Cliff's friend was a gruff, sixtyish white-skinned Creole built like a refrigerator. He had been a shipping agent in *Los Días de Somoza* but had been forced to quit his job under the Sandinistas and now built boats for a living. His name was Juan Peters-Paiz. He called the Sandinistas *hijos de puta* . . . sons of whores. "They asked me to run this town," he said. "They begged me. I turned them down, the dogs. You know they wouldn't even let me visit my sick daughter in Costa Rica."

I showed him the *Vogue*-sized sheaf and mentioned the fees.

"*Hijos de puta.*" He turned to the Customs chief. "Why do you do this? This is a *tourist.* We *need* people like this."

The Customs chief stammered and tried to explain that he

had only been following the rules. He was not a real Sandinista, after all; he was only East Indian.

"In *Los Días de Somoza*," said Peters, "these horseshit rules were waived for tourists. They simply wrote a "letter of protest" saying that they had put in for emergency. No fee, no nothing. That is what you should do now."

I qué milagro! After two hours of confabulation between the Customs chief, his deputy, and the shipping agent I'd hired ("What do we do? This man is a *tourist:* But there are no rules covering tourists."), our fee was reduced to twenty dollars, payable in traveler's checks. The sheaf of forms was presented to us free, as a gift of the government. And I assured them that this treatment would be duly mentioned in my "report."

So there it is.

DOWN AT the Seaman's Bar, Susan was talking to a man with an artificial leg and a bag of shrimp he'd tried to sell us earlier in the market. The shrimp had gone bad in the heat; you could smell them on the other side of the room.

Susan had been involved in a little drama of her own. When she'd arrived at the Seaman's Bar two hours earlier, she noticed our inflatable hull down on the horizon in the grip of the twenty-knot afternoon wind. Someone had been in it, trying to row back and getting nowhere: She'd thought it was me. Nobody on the pier seemed to notice or care.

A fisherman with an outboard-powered *cayuco* was unloading huge green turtles in the shallows at the foot of the pier. "Please," she screamed at him, pointing at the inflatable. "Look!"

After they towed him back, the shrimp-seller explained he had borrowed the inflatable to row out to the boat with the shrimp, but the wind had gotten him.

"Why did you want to take the shrimp out?"

"I thought you wanted them."

"But how could we be out there when the little boat was here?"

They'd been having the logical extension of this conversation at the table in the Seaman's Bar for the last hour and a half. We paid our check, climbed into the inflatable, and rowed away, leaving him standing on the dock holding the terrible bag of shrimp. He had tried to stop me at the last minute by grabbing my hands as I held the ropes to lower myself down. Meanwhile, a man in the crowd around us kept asking if we had a battery charger.

A NOTHER NIGHT of sleeplessness and we would have been ready to buy that bag of shrimp. Gladly. We spent the last hour of daylight putting out a stern anchor that might hold the *Lord Jim*'s bow into the swells and stop the terrible rolling. It worked better than we'd dared to hope.

To unwind, we drank good Nicaraguan *Flor de Caña* rum mixed with tamarind water (the drink of choice in these parts) and watched the sunset color the spotless white hull of the *Lady Lena*. She was now owned by the local fishing cooperative, but couldn't be used (according to Richard Benjamin) because her Caterpillar diesel had broken down, and all the Caterpillar mechanics had fled the country.

And looking out of the deckhouse at the never-changing lumpy brown swell, the pathetic cluster of fishing *cayucos,* the rusty shrimp boats, the groups of travelers lowering themselves into the sailing *cayuco* ferries, the loiterers on the high pier, the raw, red clay roads leading up past some undefined, unfinished construction project to the first line of shacks half hidden in flea-bitten undergrowth, I caught myself thinking nostalgically of the days of the British and the Mosquito Kings.

Sandinista Radio sang us to sleep. It had an English-language segment with birthday greetings for people named Wilson, Watson, Dickson, etc., announcements of community association meetings, projects, art shows, sports events ... it sounded exactly like Radio Belize, or Radio Dipstick, USA. There was some great Costeña music by Dimension Costeña from Bluefields, at first listen a mixture of punta and Miskito chants. Later, the Sandinistas got their message across in Spanish to a disco beat and the repeated phrase: *Vamos a dirijir por abajo*. We will govern from below.

We were out like a light.

R ICHARD BENJAMIN was waiting as Susan flew and I clambered up onto the pier to begin another day in Central America. He looked depressed.

"Did you ever find Steadman?"

"Steadman is not well." He tapped the left side of his chest. "Trouble here. With his heart."

I felt a strange flutter in my own heart: Just like the British before me I'd put a lot of waking energy into building my version of the man. This version felt a little like a successful classmate at St Paul's School ... a round peg in a round hole: He'd won all the prizes, graduated summa cum laude, and then while delivering the class valedictory had pulled out an AK-47. In some perverse way, I understood that I envied and admired him. Him and his beautiful wife and sister-in-law, his cozy cabin on the Cauquira waterway, his kids, his battles. And to hear about his heart trouble was as chilling as hearing about my own might be. "But he's young. How old is he, thirty-three?"

Richard Benjamin jerked his shoulders. "His life has been hard. You know."

"Where is he now?"

"He is gone. To the doctors."

"Where?"

"Where there are doctors. Not here ... Honduras, or maybe the United States."

"I'm very sorry."

"*Gracias,*" Richard Benjamin said quietly.

We stood there for a while. It was still cool, and too early for the wind. And the rocking of the pier had calmed a little too.

But Susan and I decided to leave Puerto Cabezas late that afternoon and sail to Bluefields via the Corn Islands. It was not as if we were bored in Puerto Cabezas, or thought we had seen enough. Not in the least. It was just that the anchorage was very rough, the pier was very high and splintery, and ashore things tended to ... pile up.

In the end, Steadman Fagoth was left to our imagination. Let it stand the way Orlando Roberts saw it 150 years ago ... it doesn't sound that much different:

> He (the current Mosquito King) was a young man, about twenty-four years of age, of a bright copper color, with long curly hair hanging in ringlets down the side of his face; his hands and feet small, a dark expressive eye, and very white teeth. He was an active and handsome figure, with the appearance of greater agility than strength. In other respects I found him, on further acquaintance, wild as the deer on his native savannahs. ...

ONE OF the first things you notice in the port of El Bluff, three miles across the lagoon from Bluefields, is a stranded wrecked freighter painted with Ortega's campaign slogan TODO SERÁ MEJOR. That says it all.

But if you need elaboration, there's a whole flotilla of wrecked Nicaraguan navy cutters, and a wrecked town. There is hardly a tree standing; the predominant color is gray. The only immediately visible things in decent shape are more confiscated Honduran shrimp boats. As if the place hadn't had enough trouble, the latest in a centuries-old tradition of killer hurricanes had flattened it in October 1988.

Still, compared to what we had been in recently, it was a wonderful—a heavenly—protected harbor without a wave bigger than six inches. It was early Sunday afternoon, after an easy downwind run from the Corn Islands. We were elated. Bluefields, the main Nicaraguan town on the Caribbean that more than anyplace else seemed to embody the peculiar history of the Mosquito Shore, was where we were going to make sense of it all.

B LUEFIELDS BEGAN in the seventeenth century as a buccaneer haven dominated by a Dutch pirate named Abraham Blauvelt. Along with Gracias a Dios and Black River in Honduras, it had become by the early eighteenth century one of the main settlements for planters and loggers from British Jamaica on the prowl for cheap acreage.

In the mid-nineteenth century, the British decided to move the court of the Mosquito Kingdom to Bluefields. The young boy who was to become the last British-crowned Mosquito King was taken there from his family in Gracias a Dios to be educated. He lived and studied in the household of a trader named James Stanislaus Bell: His son C. Napier Bell and the King were the same age and grew up together as brothers:

> My earliest recollections of Bluefields are those of bathing and sailing toy boats in the lagoon, and it seems to me now that a considerable part of my young days was spent in the water. My companions were the Mosquito King and coloured boys in great numbers. In the early part of the day they had to cut and split firewood, fetch water, grate cocoanuts and mind the baby. I and the King had to do our lessons, but when we had

had our dinner at one o'clock we would rush off to the lagoon, tear off our clothes, and plunge in. Then we would produce our toy boats, which were hidden in the bushes, and trimming the sails to the fresh trade wind, we launched them in batches to race, following after with shouts and yells. This was done every day during the dry season. The King and I were inseparable companions, but were not distinguished from the rest. As we grew older, the King developed the great fondness for boating which is inherent in the Mosquito Indians. Some of his relations from the Cape brought him a little canoe in the rough. It was about 10 feet long, with beam just enough to fit our little posteriors. We got it beautifully trimmed—that is, dressed down to proper shape and thickness—provided a shoulder-of-mutton sail, and sailed about the lagoon, he and I . . . (C. Napier Bell, *Tangweera: Life and Adventures Among Gentle Savages,* London, 1899)

The British, with some prodding from the United States, agreed to vacate claims to the shore in 1860 and it became a Miskito protectorate under the control of Managua. The last Mosquito King (Bell's friend) was designated head of the protectorate but when he died in 1864 without children Managua refused to extend annuities to his nephew. A year later, Bluefields was leveled yet again by the generic killer hurricane.

Still, the nephew and his descendants continued to run the protectorate, and were happy to grant favorable banana and timber concessions to American outfits in the late nineteenth century . . . after all, weren't Americans basically descended from the British? It was called the Mosquito Fruit Company, and Bluefields became a banana port.

T HE NICARAGUAN nationalist José Santos Zelaya put a stop to it. One of the first things he did on gaining power in 1893 was to occupy Bluefields with troops, declare martial law, and end the Mosquito dynasty for good: The protectorate was incorporated as a Nicaraguan state and Chief Clarence was banished to Puerto Limón, Costa Rica.

Most of the American banana community stayed on, but nationalist tariffs and controls only got worse. In the end, Bluefields was to be the center of a United States backed conservative revolution that unseated Zelaya in 1909. One of the main conservative leaders was a man called Emiliano Chamorro, a great-uncle of Violeta Chamorro's assassinated husband. So it goes.

But just as Bluefields was the center of opposition to Zelaya, so it also became the center of opposition to the conservatives. Yet another revolution broke out there in 1925, and for the second time the United States sent Marines to "protect American property."

Too bad: By the time the classic U.S. puppet Somoza came to power in 1936, most of the American property had moved on to greener pastures. All that was left of the Mosquito dynasty by the time we got there were the huge old mahogany trees—well pruned to survive the hurricane—planted in the Bluefields city park 150 years earlier in honor of the kings. And of course the feeling that after ten years of Sandinista repression another dynasty (or something comparable) would be just what the doctor ordered.

S INCE IT was Sunday afternoon, the various officials we checked in with in their hurricane-shattered offices at El Bluff were sleepy and abstracted. *No problema, señor.* The only thing we couldn't do immediately is to move the boat across the lagoon to Bluefields ... they said the channel was too shallow.

There were *cayuco* ferries across the lagoon, though, that left whenever there were enough passengers. I went over on one while Susan fell asleep to the strange, unaccustomed gentle lapping of the wavelets.

AFTER A few minutes in Bluefields, it was clearer than ever that something terribly important was to be learned here. The city was mostly bad-smelling brownish-colored rubble—a movie set for the day after World War III—but the people were happy. How could this be? It was something the British apparently learned during the bombing of London in World War II but incomprehensible to Americans, who have been through nothing worse than a few fires or earthquakes. Anyway, people were sitting around in the middle of their particular square yard of rubble looking drunk and happy. Radios were playing patois and punta all up and down the rubble-choked alleys. From the baseball stadium up the hill you could hear frantic cheering. And the particular racial potpourri of Bluefields had produced some of the most beautiful women I had ever seen, picking their way through the rubble in stiletto heels and ruffled print dresses.

Naturally we were out of cash. I walked up to a group of happily drunk men sitting outside a wrecked hotel and asked them if they knew of a place I could cash a traveler's check.

One of them leaped to his feet, put his arm around my shoulders, and told me. But he was much too drunk for me to understand.

He tried talking in English but I couldn't understand that either. Nor could he understand my Spanish or my English. In the end, all we had between us was *amistad* . . . friendship and good intentions.

"*Vamonos, gringito,*" I think he said. Let's go, little gringo. It seemed he was going to show me personally.

H E WAS a government accountant from Managua, I gathered, who had been sent to Bluefields for a couple of weeks on some job. Or he was the owner of the hotel. Or he worked in a shipping office. He looked kind of distinguished . . . or at least had a lot of Spanish (as opposed to Indian) blood. He was wearing a light yellow guayabera over brown slacks and had two big rings on two fingers of his left hand. His eyes were invisible and his lower lip was red and moist. He might have said his name was Ernesto; he was about my age. And I agreed with him every time he said we were friends.

We walked up and down the hot, bad-smelling streets for a little while, then went through an unmarked door into another dimension.

It was a big tiled room with mirrors at shoulder height above the tiles, full of well-dressed handsome people at tables being served by waiters in pressed white shirts and black bow ties. *Air conditioning.* The maîtresse d' was dressed in a beautifully fitted tuxedo and looked like Lena Horne. It reminded me a lot of Galatoire's Restaurant in New Orleans on a Friday afternoon, when the tradition is to let a lunch consume the rest of the day. But I knew it couldn't be.

My friend stood there like an owl at midday, eyes mostly closed, head tilted back, arms slightly spread out from his sides. The maîtresse d' moved toward us intimidatingly and I asked her if she could cash an American traveler's check. She shook her head.

"That's too bad," I told my friend, trying to remember my conditional and subjunctive tenses in Spanish. "If she would have cashed it, I could have bought you a beer."

Looking more owlish than ever, he motioned for me to sit

down at an empty table, spat on the tiled floor, waved the maîtresse d' over again, and asked for menus. His manner suggested
he was used to giving orders.

"No, no." I said. "I have no money. Not one córdoba."

It was like talking to the wall. I took a menu and looked at it.
It was the best looking menu I'd seen since Cozumel.

Two ice-cold Victoria beers had arrived with two ice-cold
mugs to pour them into. "Thank you very very much," I said
humbly. Meanwhile, he seemed to want me to agree (again) that
we were friends.

I was more than happy to, but must have looked rather
pathetically thirsty because another ice-cold Victoria arrived before I'd even finished the first one. I ordered the seafood chow-
der, *sopa mixta,* and when it didn't arrive almost immediately he
began to berate our waiter. "Can't you see the gringo is hungry?"
Still, that gave us time for more beers; I'm not sure how many.
And the *sopa mixta,* when it finally appeared, was the most
exquisite, delicate dish I have ever had.

C AN YOU imagine how frustrating it is to spend at least two
hours trying to thank a man who can't understand? I managed to survive the ordeal quite nicely, thank you. And he, on his
part, seemed to be doing all right, too. Meanwhile, the other
diners grew handsomer and more glamorous and I grew more
and more interested in finding out exactly where I was . . . I mean,
in the larger sense.

"Look," I told him as he paid the check. "*I* want to buy *you*
lunch here. Tomorrow." I used a lot of hand gestures and kept it
simple.

He shook his head. *"Amistad . . ."*

"Precisamente." I struggled with the conditional and

subjunctive again. "*If* you are my friend, *then* you will let me buy you lunch. Okay?"

He stared at me. Was it with comprehension?

Outside on the sidewalk we hugged each other good-bye and went in opposite directions.

WHERE WAS I? I followed one of the semipaved streets up the hill from the waterfront and turned off on a dirt side road into the back part of town. The *sopa mixta* and the Victoria beers were warming the cockles of my heart: I was in love. The ruined streets were full of lovers, flirting and strolling in their Sunday best. Wherever it was, I was in love with this place.

A TALL SLIM woman dressed in black lace came out of the door to a tin-roofed lean-to and started up the alley ahead of me. We were maybe fifty feet apart, going at about the same speed. I had not seen her face when she'd come out of the door, but from the back she looked about thirty-five: old enough to know where she was going and young enough to look very handsome while she was getting there. Her hair was black and curly, but neither short nor long and modestly restrained with pins. Her dress fit well, but not too well; it had sleeves and its back did not go below the level of her hair. The heels of her black shoes were high but not too high. One arm was crooked at the elbow: She was carrying something I couldn't see.

When she turned left at the corner up ahead, I dropped back a little so there would be less chance of her hearing my footsteps and followed her. It seemed very important: I was sure she was going to the cemetery.

A WEEK BEFORE we began the trip, we'd visited Philadelphia to say good-bye. It was a cold rainy day in late
October ... soggy leaves underfoot, light mist shading dark
branches and making them indistinct, sound of tires kissing
damp asphalt, headlights reflecting on water even though there
were two hours until sundown.

Susan stayed in the warm car in the parking lot of the
Church of the Redeemer while I wandered down between the
gravestones, looking for my mother's. It had been six years.

I had not bothered with a jacket or an umbrella because I
hadn't thought it would take long. First I tried concentric circles
from the place I'd expected to find it ... then I tried a grid system,
passing over and over again the names of many of her friends.
Nothing. It was as if it didn't exist, had never existed. After more
than an hour of searching an area that couldn't have been more
than 100 square yards I was soaked and freezing and completely
spooked. The whole thing was perfectly in the great Catherwood
tradition of silence and missed connections: When she'd died six
years earlier I had been called too late to say good-bye ... and
now I couldn't find her grave.

T HAT FALL, six years earlier, we'd been living in a rented
house near Orient on the north fork of Long Island ... just
back from a year in Mexico with a divorce trial around the
corner, two hostile teenage daughters, and no income other than
interest on a small nest egg, the pittance I could hustle from free-
lance articles, and beggings and borrowings from my mother.
"All he wants from me is my money," she'd complained several
times to friends.

Around two P.M. the phone rang. It was Trish, my father's secretary, calling from Philly. She said my mother had been in a car accident the day before and was in the hospital. It couldn't have been serious, I thought; otherwise I would have been called earlier.

"Do you think I ought to come down?"

"You probably should."

"When? Tomorrow?"

"Maybe today. If you can." It couldn't have been serious. I got to the house at about six P.M.; my father had already gone to a dinner party. When I called the hospital the nurse said my mother felt too tired to see anybody then but to come early the next day. I think I went to bed before my father got home.

We went over together the next morning, but my mother was on a respirator and couldn't talk. Her eyes were closed and she seemed only semiconscious. I called my sister in California; she was there by sundown.

We stayed in a motel near the hospital. The nurse called us to come over just before dawn. By seven o'clock the heartbeat line on the oscilloscope was flat. If it had not been for that unarguably flat line, we might have had trouble believing it even then.

THREE MONTHS later, my father remarried. It all must have been a question of keeping a stiff upper lip. Or something. I never asked him what my mother had told him before she died . . . he never offered to tell me.

But life continued almost without an interruption, except instead of living in his wife's comfortable house in Haverford, Pennsylvania, he was now living in his wife's comfortable house in Bermuda. It was all so seamless I guess it upset me . . . even though I had tried to get them together in the first place, to cheer him up. He'd just anticipated me.

And as I followed the woman in black lace around the second corner (very afraid that sooner or later she was going to discover I was following her) I realized I had some bones to pick with the old blade. I wanted to *know* what my mother had told him . . . among other things. I wanted to complain bitterly that in spite of all the charm, the delightful ornamentation, art, and adventure he had introduced me to, he remained as inscrutable as Frederick Catherwood.

As I imagined it, the cemetery where the woman was headed was the only part of Bluefields left untouched by the hurricane. There would be mahogany trees, and under them, the graves of the Mosquito Kings. She would be visiting the grave of her mother or father (I wasn't sure which) and on it she would place the flower she was carrying. She would kneel in front of it and pray . . . I'd made up my mind to kneel and pray myself.

She went across a large, rocky field of packed earth where some kids were playing soccer. I waited until she'd disappeared in the rubble on the other side and hurried across myself, while kids gathered around and measured themselves against me: "Look! I reach up to here on the gringo."

"Lend me some cacao," a kid said.

"We don't use cacao."

"What do you use?"

"Coffee and sugar."

"Well, lend me some coffee and sugar, then."

But they were laughing. I made it into the rubble where the woman had gone in time to catch that all-important glimpse of black.

CHURCH BELLS began to ring out over the wrecked town, but I was positive she wasn't going to church. The streets became more populated and it was easier to follow her unobtrusively. We passed the town pier with its pathetic cement monument to the *"Heroés y martires"* who died in the liberation of Bluefields in 1980. I worked closer to her until I could see that she wasn't wearing any stockings. She reached her left hand up and rubbed the back of her neck; I could see no wedding ring. But nobody else in the street gave her a second look, in spite of her handsomeness. It must have been the black dress . . . and the fact that she probably made the same trip every Sunday. For how long?

She stopped at a corner to let a truck go by and I got close enough to imagine I smelled perfume. It came to me that her name was María . . . that's how sappy I was getting.

Then she turned into a downtown doorway . . . apparently private: at least with no sign . . . and disappeared. The door closed (it looked like one solid piece of heavy, discolored wood) without a sound. Just like that. It was as if she had never been there. I stood in the street looking up at the windows of the house but they were either shuttered or covered with curtains. I thought about knocking on the door and almost did—*Señora, I think you dropped something*—but suddenly didn't trust myself to carry it off. I felt a little crazy . . . my eyes were prickling and stinging as if I'd been slapped. Knocking wouldn't prove anything anyway . . . except I was still positive she hadn't finished her trip.

I decided to find the cemetery myself and wait for her there. An old black guy selling what looked like bars of soap from a sidewalk stand at the next corner gave me a set of directions that I forgot almost immediately.

Then somehow I found myself back at the rocky field of packed earth; the kids were still playing soccer and were glad to see me.

"Look, the big gringo. The big gringo is back. Hey! You got Chicklets?" They seemed wild, spirited, and fearless, completely different from the snot-nosed, glue-sniffing street kids we'd been panhandled by in the big cities of Guatemala and Honduras.

Tegucigalpa had been especially nightmarish: Outside the Hotel Honduras Maya was a gauntlet of street kids who lived in the bushes and fought each other for tiny scraps of tortillas. Some had shoeshine equipment, but I never saw any of them shining shoes. They would look up at you with twisted faces and hands as black as monkeys'.

A kid kicked the ball to me or at me; I kicked it back, using the top of my right foot with a kind of sideways swing that I'd learned playing soccer at school. My left foot was still pins and needles, but if I tried really hard I found I could stand on the heel now without the toes flopping down. The kick made a solid-sounding *thock* and the ball flew hard and straight at the kid, who caught it easily on his own foot, let it bounce once, and returned it.

I trapped the ball a little clumsily and started dribbling toward the kid through a little minefield of rocks. Like magic, the others divided into two groups: one calling for the ball, one closing in on me to take it away. The pace picked up and things got easier. Soccer had been my favorite game at school, but I had been too much of a shrimp to make the varsity. Now I was at least twice the size of everybody else. And it was surprising and gratifying how many of the moves came back to me, and in fact that I seemed to be in okay shape in spite of everything.

More and more kids were trying to get the ball. It was anarchy . . . the groups broke down: everybody for himself. Finally there was only one kid left to pass it to . . . he was wearing a yellow jersey, was a little taller, and always seemed to be calling to me from an open space of ground. When my left foot finally caught on a rock and tipped me over, he left the vortex and came and sat down next to me. We were both soaked with sweat and panting. I could see his jersey had the Batman insignia on it . . . he was about eleven, with straight black hair and chocolate skin: Miskito blood.

"Okay, *tío?*" He was calling me uncle as an older guy he respects and knows well, not a relative.

"Okay. Many rocks." We grinned and shook our heads at the bad state of the playing field. He told me his name was Federico; I told him my name was Gordon, which in Spanish translates as "big fatty."

"You're not fat. How old are you?"

I decided not to lie, like I usually do, and told him the truth. It seemed very important. I was hoping he was going to be surprised, but he just nodded.

"Where did you learn *futbol?*"

"At school."

"In England."

"No, in the United States."

He did a little double take. "The United States . . . how did you get here?"

"In a boat. A sailboat."

"You sailed here in a boat?" He whistled and shook his hand as if it had been burned. *"Puta madre . . .* a big boat?"

"No. Little. Just two of us."

"Then . . . who are you?"

It was an interesting question, after all. And who would have expected to hear it come from the mouth of an eleven-year-old kid in Bluefields, Nicaragua? Even so, I couldn't answer it. "Oh, nobody."

He giggled. "No, you are somebody, *tío.* Everybody is somebody . . . for example, I am Federico."

"Then I am Gordon."

"And you must be a sailor."

I nodded. It was true.

"You're a sailor. That's why you came." He thought about it for a little while, his chin resting on his arms, which were crossed over his knees. "I want to see your boat. Will you show it to me?"

I told him we would, as soon as we got the boat to Bluefields, if I knew where to find him.

He looked surprised. "I'll watch for your boat, okay? When will you get here?"

"Maybe tomorrow."

"What time?"

"The same time." I showed him my watch. "Five o'clock."

"You'll see me waiting." He tapped himself on the chest. "Federico. That's me. And you are Gordon. Don't forget."

"I won't."

S UDDENLY IT was almost sundown: too late to find the cemetery. I didn't really want to find it anymore; I felt connected to the world for the first time in quite a while. Things seemed sharp and clear the way I remembered they'd felt twenty years ago: like an Eliot Porter photograph.

I was alive. Wringing out my sweat-wet shirt I hurried back down the slimy alleys to the *cayuco* landing hoping I wasn't too late for the last cayuco to El Bluff.

The lights were on in the *Lord Jim* when I got there and Susan was cooking up a batch of fresh shrimp that the Colombian crew of the American-owned shrimp boat anchored downwind had given us. She looked rested and happy and very beautiful.

"So how was Bluefields?"

"Very lively."

She looked more closely and giggled. "Your shirt's a mess and you're all dirty. You look like a grubby little boy. What are you grinning about?"

M Y MUSCLES started to stiffen up after dinner . . . I was good and tired after all. Stretching felt terrific. I went up into the wheelhouse, did a few exercises, and looked at the dim lights of Bluefields across the lagoon.

Give me two weeks here, and I'll have things wired. Now that I know how to look at them.

THE SANDINISTA bureaucracy was back on the job early Monday morning: Not only could we not take the *Lord Jim* across the lagoon to the town, we would need to get special permission ourselves each time we wanted to go. Plus, we'd have to hire another shipping agent. When we refused to do this a second time Señor Bilches of *migración* conveniently noticed that our visa had not been used within the proper period.

We were quarantined on the ship while he conferred with superiors, then we were told to get out of Nicaragua. A sad little burlesque followed over the exit fee of twenty-five dollars, for which they refused to accept a traveler's check.

"Well," I said, "If I wasn't quarantined, maybe I could get it cashed in Bluefields."

They thought about that for a little while, then agreed to let me go. Since there were no *cayucos* leaving at that moment I had to take the little inflatable. Roaring across the lagoon at full speed, my head full of plans to take our case to higher authorities and the newspapers, I got careless and took my hand off the outboard tiller for a second. The boat flipped. I came up out of the four-foot-deep brown water to see the propeller of the outboard whirling against the gray sky.

A PASSING *cayuco* full of laughing Cubans helped me right the inflatable and towed me back to the *Lord Jim*, where I struggled to disassemble and flush out the outboard before it was permanently ruined. The VHF started spitting at us. It sounded like Señor Bilches.

"I can't talk to you now," I yelled into the microphone. "It's an emergency. The boat turned over and I have to work on the motor."

"In that case, we'll accept the traveler's checks."

He came out in the official tender to get them, and had the grace to look a little embarrassed.

Susan was very angry. "We came as friends, and we will leave as friends. But you make it difficult, señor."

"Maybe we'll see you in New York sometime," I told him.

He shook our hands, slapped me on the shoulder, and blushed. *"Es posible."*

Five

Reprise: Points South

HRISTOPHER COLUMBUS talked to the natives of Central America in sign language, holding his hands up a few inches apart to indicate a strait, the passage through to China and the Indies: fame and all the untold riches that Marco Polo had raved about 200 years earlier. But the natives thought he meant an isthmus, not a strait. They smiled, nodded, and made the same gesture: yes, yes. Right around the corner, Very narrow.

The place that Columbus led himself to believe was the object of his search is a 100-foot-wide shallow channel leading from one coastal lagoon to another in Panama, just south of the Costa Rican border. From the old banana port of Bocas del Toro, where Columbus stopped to careen his ships and pump the natives, it does appear as a tiny break in an otherwise unbroken coast. And the natives were quick to agree that it was in fact the way through . . . which it was. Now they call it Split Hill Channel, between Bahía Almirante and Chiriquí Lagoon.

The closer you get, the more it looks like what Columbus was praying for . . . even *we* got pretty excited . . . until you come out in a wide, landlocked bay with a chain of mountains to the west and you realize it's just more of the same. Laguna de Chiriquí was where Columbus abandoned all hope of finding the strait, and decided to concentrate instead on local gold: *"Oh, most excellent gold! Who has gold has a treasure with which he gets what he wants, imposes his will on the world, and even helps souls to paradise."*

But Central America, as later generations of exploitation chiefs found out, was not to be known for its untold riches. A year or so later Columbus was on his way back to Spain ... poorer and wiser and very unsure he was going to make it at all. For some reason ...

> Let those who are fond of blaming and finding fault, while they sit safely at home, ask, "Why did you not do thus and so?" I wish they were on this voyage; I well believe that another voyage of a different kind awaits them, or our faith is naught.

... he had neglected to tar his ships against the wood-boring teredo worms. One ship had to be abandoned on the Panama coast and the other two were in such bad shape that *"all the people with pumps, kettles and other vessels were insufficient to bail out the water that entered by the wormholes."* (from *The Narrative of Diego Mendez*). Columbus, in fact, couldn't even make it to Hispaniola in the Swiss-cheesed ships but was forced to run them ashore on a deserted beach in Jamaica where he and his men sat for a year waiting for rescue and he wrote his pathetic *Lettera Rarissima* to the Sovereigns.

This document (which the above quotes came from) deserves a little attention. It sets the tone for quite a few future ventures in the area:

> When I discovered the Indies, I said they were the world's wealthiest realm. I spoke of gold, pearls, precious stones, spices and of the markets and fairs. But, because not everything turned up at once, I was vilified ...
>
> I came to serve you at the age of twenty-eight (*sic*) and now I have not a hair on me that is not white, and my body is infirm and exhausted. All that was left to me and my brothers

has been taken away and sold, even to the cloak that I wore, without hearing or trial, to my great dishonor ...

The honest purpose which I have always shown in Your Highnesses' service, coupled with such unmerited outrage, will not permit my soul to keep silent, even though I might so desire. I implore your Highnesses' pardon. I am ruined, as I have said. Hitherto I have wept for others; now, Heaven have pity on me, and earth, weep for me! Of things material I have not a single *blanca* to offer; of things spiritual, I have even ceased observing the forms, here in the Indies. Alone, desolate, infirm, daily expecting death, surrounded by a million savages full of cruelty and our enemies, and thus deprived of the Holy Sacraments of Holy Church, how neglected will this soul be if here it part from the body! Weep for me, whoever has the charity, truth and justice! I did not come on this voyage for gain, honor or wealth, that is certain; for then the hope of all such things was dead. I came to Your Highnesses with honest purpose and zeal; and I do not lie ...

WE WERE feeling sorry for ourselves too, after getting thrown out of Nicaragua. But unlike Columbus and the rest (I thought bitterly) what we had hoped to take away with us would not have subtracted one lousy córdoba from the country's reserves ... hell, it might even have added some, although I wasn't sure how.

We'd come there on an honorable quest, only to run afoul of an asshole named Bilches who (after all) was trying to revenge himself for yet another barefaced act of intervention. We were on his side, but he was too much of an asshole to see it. It was downright ironic.

And yet ...

"But I didn't come on any quest," Susan said.

I stared at her with a sinking heart.

"Don't look at me that way."

"Well, why did you come then? And don't give me any shit about 'I did it all for you.'"

"I just wanted to *see* it. I wanted to *do* it. Isn't that enough?" She was starting to get angry.

After five months of looking for things I couldn't quite close my fingers on even when I found them, the only answer I could come up with was "Maybe it is." I didn't actually say it until a few hours later, when we were well underway from Bluefields to Puerto Limón, Costa Rica.

But it was that simple. As soon as I said it, I felt we were off the hook. We were out of the cycle.

We were free.

ON THE lobster shift (midnight to four A.M.) with a half moon outside the wheelhouse lighting up a few of the wavetops, one of those unexplainable memory loops started up in my head. It was an excerpt from that old preacher John Donne's *Meditations* that my father had kept under the glass top of his desk for as long as I'd been able to read—the whole goddamn excerpt, not just a snatch of it. He'd made me memorize it once as a punishment for something:

No man is an *Iland*,
Intire of it selfe;
Every man is a peece of the *Continent*,
A part of the *maine*;
If a *Clod* bee washed away by the *Sea*,
Europe is the lesse,
As well as if a *Promontorie* were,
As well as if a *Mannor* of thy *friends*
Or of *thine owne* were;
Any mans *death* diminishes *me*,

Because I am involved in *Mankinde*;
And therefore never send to know
For whom the *bell* tolls;
It tolls for *thee*.

It occurred to me then, for the first time, that my father actually believed this and in fact might even have lived by it.

But there was another excerpt under the glass that I could recite from memory too, even though he'd never forced me to memorize it:

The sun was warm but the wind was chill.
You know how it is with an April day
When the sun is out and the wind is still,
You're one month on in the middle of May.
But if you so much as dare to speak,
A cloud comes over the sunlit arch,
A wind comes off a frozen peak,
And you're two months back in the middle of March.
　　　　　　　　　　　　　　　—Robert Frost

Something else has just this moment occurred to me: The accomplishment and discoveries of the cruise of the *Lord Jim* might be mine, but if he hadn't showed me what he had I wouldn't be writing about them.

I wouldn't be writing at all. Any flair for words I might have developed began the day he opened my first grade reader (*"Oh my," said Dick. "See Spot run!"*), crossed out the "Oh my" and wrote in "Odds bodkins!"

PUERTO LIMÓN, in Costa Rica, is described in most guide-books as a "typical Somerset Maugham port town," meaning seedy. But Nicaragua had added new dimensions to the word, and in Puerto Limón harbor we felt like we had dropped anchor in Beverly Hills. Like refugees, we gawked around the office of the *Capitania del Puerto: "Look, electric typewriters. Computers. Xerox machines. Air conditioners."*

There were trees in the parks (with tame sloths hanging in them, even), almost no rubble, paved roads with cars on them, produce in the markets. The sight of things like refrigerators, stoves, television sets, and washing machines gleaming new in one department store actually brought tears to Susan's eyes . . .

I T WAS perhaps inevitable that in a place like this, a place of good times and plenty, that we were to come across the latest (not the last) of the breed . . . although one would hesitate to call him a direct descendant of Columbus.

He called himself Charley Tuna. We first noticed him in The American Cafe, a sidewalk hot spot across from the wonderfully overgrown park: a tall, muscley guy with pale blond hair down to his shoulders, shades and an earring and a T-shirt cut away under the arms to show his build. He was hard to miss. *"Look! Hulk Hogan."* And we were sure, too, that he was from our country.

We saw him again later that evening, having dinner in the restaurant of the Hotel Acon, downstairs from the disco. He was with another gringo and a frizzy-haired, beefy Ladino. We overheard snatches of conversation: "I ran for president of my union, man, but the blacks just used me. They said they were behind me, but they were just using me to split the fucking vote so they could get their man in."

Toward the end of the meal, the young, handsome waitress began trying to tell the gringos something in Spanish, but they didn't understand. She was pointing at the Costa Rican with them and her lip was curled. They shrugged and grinned. Her voice rose. We could overhear words like *rata, ladrón, malo.* Rat. Thief. Bad.

"She doesn't seem to like you, buddy," said the blond man, who was wearing a Charley the Tuna hat and had a gold Charley the Tuna charm around his neck on a chain.

When they left, we asked the waitress what the problem was. Her eyes flashed: "I try to warn everybody about that man. He hustles gringos, gets them drunk, and takes their money. Says he'll get them girls and then robs them. *Una rata.* But they didn't understand."

"I think they got the idea."

THE NEXT night we ran into them again, having dinner in a Chinese place. Charley Tuna's friend was very drunk, down on his hands and knees trying to feed his dinner to a little dog. But the dog kept barking at him.

I went over to the table. Close up, Charley Tuna looked older than he had from a distance.

"You know that waitress last night," I said. "She was trying to tell you you were in bad company."

Charley Tuna grinned. "Aw, he only got me for about five dollars." He had a friendly—even winsome—grin, with good white teeth. He took off his shades and his eyes were electric blue, like Nick Nolte's . . . he actually looked much more like Nolte than Hulk Hogan. Soon we were sitting at his table.

"Why do they call you Charley Tuna?" Susan asked, after he had introduced himself.

He flashed his grin and rolled his eyes. "Because I taste good."

"Oh."

"Naw . . . because he smells like one." Charley Tuna's new friend Dan had been in Costa Rica for three weeks, working for his brother who repaired ship containers. But he had been on a little vacation with Charley Tuna for the last few days.

C HARLEY TUNA turned out to be a shockingly well preserved fifty-one. His secret was Lubriderm skin lotion twice a day on face, hands, and elbows. No soap on his face—ever. Also tanning for one hour on each side and thirty minutes on his back, well coated with mineral oil. He was a retired longshoreman from Houston, Texas, with a pension of $1,200 a month plus full medical. As a sideline, he designed custom cars (he had pictures of eight of them—including one shaped like a Maltese Cross, and a gold velour chariot "like in *Ben Hur*"). He also had a "tent business," catering to state fairs, weddings, etc. His last state fair was Monroe County's, in Key West. He said he did that every year because he loved Key West. Had I seen him before?

He was visiting every province in Costa Rica, and keeping a journal that he planned to turn into a book.

"Do you mind if I put you in it?"

"Not if I can put you in mine."

A ND, LIKE Columbus, like Henry Morgan, like William Walker, like Stephens and Catherwood, like Sam (the Banana Man) Zemurray, like O. Henry . . . *like us* . . . Charley Tuna had a quest. He was looking for something to take back with him . . . except in his case it was actually *someone.*

First he tried Belize, but everybody in Belize turned out to be black . . . and Charley Tuna has had enough trouble with the blacks in the Longshoremen's Union to turn him off them for a lifetime . . . even though some of his best friends are black.

Then someone told him about Costa Rica, where the people are lighter in color than any other country in Central or South America with the exception (maybe) of Argentina.

"She's got to be fourteen or less. No older. That's against the law in Texas . . . I mean, serious time. Of course, sometimes I got by with it—I mean, I might have a girlfriend with a niece or someone who'd say go ahead. Rape?? *Never.*" He grins. "I'm only as bad as they'll let me be."

He pulls a picture from his wallet: a smiling country girl. "Seventeen. We have a son now, I'll be seeing him first thing when I get back . . . she says he's blond, like me, but not as good-looking. *Naturally* (grins). And I've got two boys with my ex-wife . . . I built her a nice house (shows picture) and we're still friends, except she went through the change of life and kind of lost interest in that side of things. Finally threw me out . . . see, I need to get a little at least once a day. Nossir, never a day gone by since I was thirteen . . ."

"Now, if I find someone here, I'm going to be real nice to her . . . I'll set her up in a nice place, pay all her bills, everything. And it'll be better than she ever lived before in her life."

S USAN DIDN'T buy my line of reasoning that in his own way Charley Tuna was no different than us. We said good-bye and headed for the door just as the television set erupted in a Ninja battle . . . screams, groans, grunts, the sound of blows. "Hey, that sounds like an X-rated movie," Dan was saying. And Charley Tuna's eyes popped wide open in appreciation and he roared with laughter.

I TOOK A magical little train up to the capital of San José to get new parts made for the autopilot, cash traveler's checks, etc., while Susan recuperated from Nicaragua on the *Lord Jim.* The train never went faster than twenty miles an hour, swaying through groves of bamboo and clouds of butterflies (brushing against and flying in through the open windows) while children in blue-and-white school uniforms jumped on and off. Two Norwegian medical students and I compared impressions ... "The train is dancing, etc." ... meanwhile, unknown to me, Charley Tuna was in another car writing up his notes. It seemed we were fated to be together. I helped him give directions to a cab driver in San José and we agreed to meet later at a bar called Happy Days. He winked: "Happy Nights would be more like it."

Things hadn't really started to roll at Happy Days when I got there a little after six P.M. A few Costa Rican girls were gathered on one side of the big rectangular bar, talking and laughing, and a few gringos were beginning to collect along the other. The girls were flashy and self-conscious and the gringos seemed elderly. The decor was a Costa Rican fantasy of what it must be like in a roadhouse in Charley Tuna's hometown of Houston, Texas ... a suggestion of sin, but nothing too expensive. Charley Tuna was by himself down at the end, almost hidden behind a huge pile of T-shirts, his white hair glowing in the gloom.

He held one up: it said HAPPY DAYS. "I got sixty of these for the fans at home, but that's not as many as I got last year at Indianapolis." He pulled a necklace of painted wooden beads from his pocket. "Got a few of these, too. Give this to Susan for me, okay? Last Christmas I spent $200 on stuff like this ... all for women."

The lady bartender abstractedly brought us two beers. "So tell me," I said. "Have you had any *luck* here? I mean, uh, what have you *come up* with? Speaking of women."

"In here? Baby, I never pay for it if I can get it for free. I don't patronize this place, I just feel comfortable here."

"No, I meant *in general.*"

He shook his head sadly. "Nada. Nada thing. No luck ... they all need two bar stools."

"I don't believe it. How long have you been here?"

"Almost a month, baby."

"Come on, Charley. You're holding out on me."

"God's truth. Would I lie to a fellow American?"

"Aw, come on, Charley."

W E SAT there nursing our beers and watching the action slowly begin to gather speed. The bar lady drifted down and I ordered two more beers . . . when she brought them we had a little conversation in Spanish, mostly about the weather.

After she left, Charley Tuna's eyes were strangely thoughtful. "You speak pretty good, don't you? I forgot."

"Well, I can get by."

"Maybe running into you was my lucky day."

This was a little alarming to hear, considering. But I smiled and asked him why.

He had found her all right, but there was a problem: They couldn't understand each other. At all. She didn't speak a word of English, he didn't speak Spanish. And the generation gap was there, too—almost two generations. She worked as a waitress in a restaurant around the corner where her mother was a cook . . . her mother didn't speak English either and seemed kind of cool to Charley Tuna.

"Her name's Teresa. You ought to see her face light up whenever I come in. She's crazy about me."

"How long has this been going on?"

"Since before I went to Limón."

"Why did you go to Limón if you'd already found her?"

"Had to. I had to get out of town. It was driving me crazy."

I didn't want any part of helping him in his peculiar quest, God knows, but it occurred to me that if I didn't do it someone else would. And, if I went along with him, it was just possible that

I could have some . . . influence. So I agreed at least to go to the restaurant and meet the girl.

A T FOURTEEN, to gringo eyes, Latin American girls are at their all-time best . . . rangy, wild, careless, impudent . . . and totally out of reach. They wear heartbreakingly demure school jumpers during the day and go around in laughing groups but under their thick, dark eyelashes their eyes are flashing with promise and potential that only a handful of them are ever able to live up to.

Teresa had a dimple in one corner of her mouth, and was modestly sassy in her way of asking us what we wanted to eat, but that's as far as it seemed to go. Well, she did know his name. For the rest, she was a typical Latin American fourteen-year-old girl. She was wearing stone-washed designer jeans instead of a dress. And she might have known also that she took our breath away.

"What do you want me to say?"

He drew himself up and smiled his most winsome smile: "Just tell her that . . . I like her a lot . . . and that I want to be her, uh . . ."

The word that came to mind was *novio,* sweetheart. I pushed it out immediately. *Amigo* was what I said to her. Friend. He wants to be your friend. Your American friend.

Her reaction was stunning, even for me. She caught her tongue between her teeth and giggled with no sign of surprise whatsoever. Her accent was heartbreaking. She leaned over and slapped him lightly on the back of his hand. Then she walked away, giggling at us over her shoulder, and leaving her words hanging there in the air above the table:

"Sorry, Charley."

YOU KNOW I couldn't feel sorry for him, even though at that moment he looked a little like Columbus must have looked when he realized he was never going to make it through to the Pacific. On the contrary: It was pretty exhilarating. This girl had served up with an enviable spirit and insouciance 500 years of very questionable history. It was enough to make a person think that everything was going to turn out for the best.

THANKS TO the Industrial Revolution and an heroic measure of gringo intervention, Columbus's long-sought passage through to the Pacific now exists. We arrived at the outer breakwater of the Panama Canal just before dawn, and the city lights I had been steering by for the last couple hours turned out to belong to fifteen huge freighters anchored off. We wallowed around in the confused backwash from the breakwater and finally, as the sun roared up over the edge of where we had been for the past five months, passed between the blinking green and red lights into calm water.

We didn't take the sails down right away . . . that seemed a little drastic because, after all, when were we going to put them up again? The *Lord Jim* eased along a little to starboard of the main channel while the VHF spat at us in at least ten different languages and freighters moved silently through the low hills in front of us with twentieth century inevitability. The invasion was four months in the past, Noriega was preparing his defense in custody of the USA, and here at the Canal it seemed to be business as usual.

The yacht anchorage was in a little cove just past some huge old Gothic piers. The shore was too low and marshy for buildings . . . just reeds, royal palms, and, farther back, tall trees. It was absolutely quiet: The little dawn breeze had dropped to nothing and everybody was still asleep.

The other yachts looked very salty, with self-steering gear, wind generators, fuel cannisters, man-overboard buoys, heavy-duty dodgers, baggy-wrinkles, life rafts . . . all of them well-used, none of them shiny, some of them downright dilapidated. They looked as different from the spick-and-span craft you see in the fancy marinas as . . . well . . . as we ourselves did. Susan took the helm and maneuvered while I dropped anchor next to an old wooden schooner flying the French tricolor and watched a naked man wander sleepily on deck, stretch, and take the first piss of the day. He turned, saw us watching, grinned and waved and went back below. Then we took our sails down, Susan furling the mizzen, me the main. As usual.

We worked slowly together, not wanting to rush through it. For sailors the Canal means the end, but it also means the beginning. We were both starting to realize that the cruise of the *Lord Jim* had in fact barely begun, but it did feel as if something had already been accomplished. Among other things, an eleven-year-old boy in Bluefields, Nicaragua (the seediness capital of the world), had told me my name and my vocation.

We coiled the lines and got the boat shipshape and ready for land. Then we sat in our cockpit side by side, a little bit shy with each other now that we were pretty sure about the way it was going to be, and watched the other boat people begin to wake up.

Coda

OAT PEOPLE. In the early afternoon, after a nap, we dinghied in to the decrepit Panama Canal Yacht Club just in time to catch the dock lines of a trim thirty-seven-foot Crealock double-ended cutter out of Seattle, Washington. A mid-fiftyish man at the helm was giving orders to a young couple on the foredeck, who were obeying them with lightninglike speed and impressive efficiency. They were both calling him Dad. I thought of how our own trip would have been with my father on board in the flesh instead of only in my memories and knew I had to learn their story.

When the boat was secure, the brother and sister (both husky and blond and somewhere in their twenties) helped their father ashore. His face was tanned but grayish and his eyes were squinting in pain but he spoke heartily of their trip south, which had taken the better part of a year.

"Where do you go from here?"

"Europe!" He said it in a way that made me want to help him get there myself.

THE STORY was short and simple: We got it from the brother a few nights later, while the sister took her father to dinner downtown at the Hotel Washington.

They were a sailing family. The father started them early, in little twelve-foot Turnabouts on Buzzards Bay. There was a big class at the local yacht club, lots of races: The brother and sister, sailing together, won the championship two years running. Meanwhile the parents were racing Luders 16s: small, full-keeled sloops that looked like miniature America's Cup contenders from the fifties.

When the brother was twelve and the sister ten their parents "split up." The brother was careful not to assign blame: After all, it was a time when everybody was doing it. Their father went to live in Seattle (the brother did not say why, or with whom) and they stayed with their mother in Massachusetts. They didn't see much of their father after that at all. They went off to top colleges, got jobs in New York City, but neither of them had steady love interests and had not considered marriage. Their jobs sounded impressive but impermanent: He was a "market analyst," she was a "sales consultant."

Last year, they both got copies of the same fifteen-page letter from their father in Seattle. He had terminal cancer; doctors gave him three to six months to live. He wanted to take a last voyage, and he wanted it to be with his son and daughter. He took fourteen pages to explain exactly why and how much he needed them. And he said he was going to call in a week to find out what they wanted to do.

The brother and sister spent the week arguing. "We don't owe him a goddamn thing," the sister said. "He walked out on us." The brother said he could see her point but wanted to go anyway . . . for their own benefit. "It will be our last chance to know him." There was never a question of one going without the other.

The point that carried was that the voyage would only last for six months, and probably a lot less. They could get leaves of absence from their jobs and sublet their apartments. When the father called they said yes; the sister half because she owed it to her brother . . . who had in fact taken her father's place all during her adolescence.

The father flew them to Seattle to help pick out the boat which they would be inheriting. They agreed with no argument on the well-used Crealock . . . after all, they had the same background and taste. Then they flew back to New York to arrange their affairs while the father sold his house and set the boat up for the trip. There didn't seem to be a woman in his life, which surprised them now that they thought about it.

T HEY LEFT Seattle in early spring, weathering a four-day gale off Mendocino in which the boat rode twenty-foot breaking seas like a duck. And they both had a hard time smiling when their father said she was seaworthy enough to go around the world.

After three months of slow, easy sailing in the summer trades they were anchored in La Paz harbor near the southern tip of Baja California. The temperature was well over 100 during the day and they watched their father carefully . . . he seemed more healthy now than when they'd begun. On a hot, dry evening with the water of the harbor glowing vermilion from the clouds, they toasted one another with margaritas on the balcony of Fulano's Restaurant and decided to cruise up into the remote islands south of Loreto in the Sea of Cortés . . .

A T THE end of six months, they were back in La Paz, back at Fulano's, facing another round of margaritas.

The father raised his glass. "To the Canal."

S O HERE you are," Susan said.

"Yep."

"On your way to Europe."

"Uh huh."

"How long will that take, do you think?"

"It could take another year."

"How's your father?" I asked.

"He has good days and bad days, but overall he's about the same now as when we left."

"Has he been to any doctors?"

"Nope. He says the sea is his doctor." He laughed.

"What about your jobs and your apartments?"

"We just keep extending the subleases. That's pretty easy in New York. The jobs?" He laughed again. "Well, the kind of jobs we had aren't that hard to find. If you're qualified. Which we are."

"And this is a once-in-a-lifetime opportunity, isn't it?" Susan said.

He laughed and nodded. "You said it."

I went and refilled our glasses. We were finishing up the last of our Nicaraguan rum, mixed with Coke. I thought of how to phrase all the questions I needed to ask and came up with nothing graceful at all. Nothing more than "How's it been so far?" as I put the full glass in front of him.

He took a long, thoughtful drink, tilted his head back, and closed his eyes for a second. "Oh, just great," he said. I could hear my own father, repeating clearly in his British accent one of his favorite maxims: *You can't have your cake and eat it, too.* It was just possible, I thought, that we had proved him wrong.

Fin

My father died on April 14, 1991, suddenly of a ruptured aneurism. At that time, this book was still in manuscript; he had not read it. I was waiting to give it to him in its final form.

Selected Bibliography

PERSONAL

W. H. Auden and Christopher Isherwood. *Journey to a War,* Paragon House. New York, 1990 (original edition New York, 1939).

'Graham Greene. *Journey Without Maps.* William Heinemann Ltd. London, 1936.

Peter Matthiessen. *Wildlife in America.* Viking Press. New York, 1959.

Eric Muspratt. *Going Native.* Michael Joseph Ltd. London, 1936.

William S. Porter. *The Complete Works of O. Henry.* Doubleday, Page & Co. New York, 1927.

Jonathan Raban, *Coasting: A Private Voyage.* Simon and Schuster. New York, 1987.

William Albert Robinson. *Deep Water and Shoal.* New York, 1932.

Robert Stone. *A Flag For Sunrise.* Alfred A. Knopf. New York, 1981.

HISTORICAL

Samuel A. Bard (E. G. Squier). *Waikna: Adventures on the Mosquito Shore.* Harper & Brothers. New York, 1855.

C. Napier Bell. *Tangweera: Life and Adventures among Gentle Savages.* University of Texas Press. Austin, 1989 (original edition, London 1899).

Craig L. Dozier. *Nicaragua's Mosquito Shore: The Years of British and American Presence.* University of Alabama Press. 1985.

SELECTED BIBLIOGRAPHY

John Esquemeling. *The Buccaneers of America.* Dover Publications. New York, 1967 (original edition Amsterdam, 1678).

Samuel Eliot Morison. *Admiral of the Ocean Sea: A Life of Christopher Columbus.* Little Brown and Co. Boston, 1942.

————. *Journals and Other Documents in the Life and Voyages of Christopher Columbus.* Heritage Press. New York, 1963.

Franklin Parker ed. *Travels in Central America 1821–1840.* University of Florida Press. Gainesville, 1970.

Orlando W. Roberts. *Voyages and Excursions on the East Coast and in the Interior of Central America.* University of Florida Press. Gainesville, 1965 (original edition Edinburgh, 1827).

C. Alphonso Smith. *O. Henry.* Chelsea House. New York, 1980.

E. G. Squier. *Nicaragua: Its People, Scenery and Monuments.* D. Appleton & Co. New York, 1851.

John L. Stephens. *Incidents of Travel in Central America, Chiapas and Yucatan.* Harper and Brothers. New York, 1841.

Victor Wolfgang von Hagen. *Frederick Catherwood, Archt.* Oxford University Press. New York, 1950.

————. *Maya Explorer: John Lloyd Stephens and the Lost Cities of Central America and Yucatan.* University of Oklahoma Press. 1947.

POLITICAL

George Black. *Good Neighbors: How the United States Wrote the History of Central America and the Caribbean.* Pantheon Books. New York, 1988.

Christopher Dickey. *With the Contras.* Simon and Schuster. New York, 1985.

Steadman Fagoth. *La Moskitia: Lamento indigena.*

Walter LaFeber. *Inevitable Revolutions: The United States in Central America.* W.W. Norton & Co. New York, 1984.

SELECTED BIBLIOGRAPHY

RECREATIONAL

Hilary and George Bradt. *Backpacking in Central America.* Bradt Enterprises. Boston, 1979.

Jeremy Hart and William T. Stone. *A Cruising Guide to the Caribbean and the Bahamas.* G. P. Putnam's Sons. New York, 1982.